ATTRACTION DECODED

30 Days
to *Transform* Your Dating Life
Boost, Your Confidence,
and *Reclaim* Your Masculinity

Copyright © 2019 by Michael Valmont

All rights reserved to the author
No part of this book may be reproduced, scanned, or distributed in any manner whatsoever without written permission from the author except in the case of brief quotation embodied in critical articles and reviews.

CONTENTS

INTRODUCTION 1

CHAPTER ONE 9
   You Will Cultivate a Positive State and Invest In Yourself Every Day 9
      Feed Your Mind with Empowering, Positive Information 19
      Harsh Truth 28
      Action Steps 30

CHAPTER TWO 33
   You Will Tackle Fear and Anxiety Head On 33
      Action Steps 44

CHAPTER THREE 45
   You Will Look and Feel Your Best Every Day 45
      Start Working Out 47
      Change Your Diet 49
      Grooming and Style 54
      Some other quick style tips: 57
      Action Steps: 58

CHAPTER FOUR 59
   You Will Focus On Your Ultimate Vision and Be Purposeful 59
      Action Steps 71

CHAPTER FIVE 73
   You Will Not Watch Porn Every Day 73
      Action Steps 76

CHAPTER SIX 77

   You Will Stop Drinking Alcohol Every Day 77

      Action Steps 81

CHAPTER SEVEN 83

   You Will Proactively Build Your Social and Dating Life 83

      Smile 107

      Vocal Use 108

      Physicality 109

      Action Steps 121

FINAL CHAPTER 123

   Conclusion and Challenge 123

   Next Steps 129

   Get In Contact 131

   About the Author 133

INTRODUCTION

You've been lied to.

There is no simple formula to attract women. No perfect trick that'll get her to drop her panties and clamor for your affection.

This book shines a light on the truth of what it takes to get what you want from your dating life.

It is my personal rebellion against poor dating advice that proliferates in magazines, videos and books and has left you wondering why you aren't dating the beautiful women in the world.

Let me explain.

There are two types of terrible dating advice.

The first piece of advice: 'be yourself'.

Let's face it, being told to be yourself feels good, and it's easy to say, but it isn't helpful. This type of advice is terrible because it doesn't encourage growth or effort. It lets you off the hook, when in reality, if you aren't having success with women, changing yourself is perhaps the best place to start.

The second piece of advice: get aggressive.

This implies tricks or gimmicks. Sure, tactics like these that pickup gurus often propagate can work, but they are usually the exception, not the rule.

You may even sleep with some women, but the change never lasts. When it stops, you search for the next self-development 'fix', looking for the next nugget of advice that might save your failing dating life. I have worked with or met nearly all the top dating coaches in the world, and listen closely when I say this:

A lot of the dating coaching industry is the 'blind leading the blind'. These so-called coaches are not usually fulfilled; they struggle to build lasting relationships and loving bonds.

So what do they do?

Well, they teach *you*. You learn their ways and methods. You may even learn a trick or two and get laid as a result.

But no matter how many regurgitated tactics or techniques you learn, it's still ultimately not going to help you attract women in a sustainable way – a 'method' that you can use in a year's time or 20 years down the line. What you'll be learning in this book is much less about method and more about principle.

So, "How do I attract women?" you ask?

I get asked this question by guys all the time, whether it's from a client I'm coaching, in the comments section on my YouTube channel, or an email in my inbox.

It's the #1 question I get asked and my answer is always the same:

Attraction is not about what you do. It's about *who you are*.

The dating gurus mentioned above think that attracting women is like checking off boxes on a list (in the pickup community, they use a *literal* list), or if they follow a series of seduction techniques, amazing women will flock to them in droves.

I can give you the perfect opening line, show you how to make subtle physical contact, or use body language to your advantage, but if the essence of *who you are* does not match the person you're making yourself out to be, she will see straight through the bullshit and move on to someone who does.

My name is Michael Valmont, and I'm going to show you the core habits and proven steps I used to transform myself from a shy, introverted kid with zero skills with women into a confident, charismatic, masculine man in the world.

Getting better with women is simple – really, it is — but it is not easy.

This is NOT a simple 'How To' guide of checklists and cheesy pickup lines. The truth is, the success you'll experience after reading this book won't come overnight.

But that's actually a good thing.

Rather than rolling the dice on predatory, ineffective pickup techniques, what if you could develop the habits and attributes that women are biologically hard-wired to find irresistible?

Is that something you might be interested in?

You see, you think you want to be *effective with women*, but what you're really interested in – even if you don't realize it — is becoming more *effective as a man.*

Sure, being ripped like Ryan Reynolds and charismatic like Clooney are attractive to many, *many* women, but what ALL women are deeply attracted to is a man who is effective in the world.

Being in shape is fantastic, and you should work on it if you've been slacking at the gym, but attraction is about more than just looks.

Building strength of character, confidence, mastering your mind, and becoming a better, more authentic version of yourself are the core attributes that will radically improve your attractiveness. And all of these things can be achieved with the right mindset and the right habits.

It took me years of pain, frustration, and anger to realize that these were the habits and attributes that lead to results.

At first I thought my happiness and confidence were the result of seeing some success with women, but eventually I realized my success with women was the result of the habits that brought me happiness and confidence in the first place.

These habits will be your core foundation in becoming an effective man in the world.

If you follow them, you will become happier, more confident, and able to succeed at anything you put your mind to. You will naturally attract the right women for you, and you can stop wasting your time and energy exclusively trying to pick up women in environments that simply don't work for you. It will allow you to focus on your strengths and not get sucked into short-term strategies or tactics that are ineffective for you.

To become the man that women want will require some work. Building new habits that will support you while eliminating ones that hold you back will be difficult at first. It will require discipline, but that's just part of the game – a game you can win if you understand the rules.

After working with thousands of guys, I've heard the same excuses over and over again.

I "want" to approach women, but…

I "want" to wake up earlier, but…

I "want" to start a business, but…

I "want" to go to the gym and get in good shape, but…

This book is about turning those wants into MUSTs.

Because we don't get what we WANT in life. We get what we MUST have. And once you tell yourself this the next step is to set new standards for yourself, get in the game, and actually start DOING.

This program is about replacing bad habits with good ones. Bad habits like jerking off to porn instead of meeting real women or hitting the snooze button every morning instead of getting up and getting after it.

These bad habits may give you momentary pleasure, but you know deep down that they are holding you back from reaching your potential.

It's time to change all of that through applying these habits.

Once you start implementing them, these cornerstone habits will become part of your daily routine and then deeply embodied in who you are.

People will marvel at you and ask *how the hell did he manage to have the discipline to become such a well-rounded person.* You'll smile because you'll know the truth.

The truth that discipline = freedom.

It will require effort, yes, but if you're reading this, you're playing the long game. No gimmicks or tricks, but proven habits that will help you become the man women talk about when they hopelessly wonder, "*Where are all the good men in the world?*"

This book will help you become that man.

This is certainly not a 'one size fits all' program. From my experience, dating coaches and companies assume what works for them works for you. Most of it is regurgitated, rehashed advice from guys that have not walked the walk.

My strategy is a lot more personalized and takes into account your special strengths, preferences, and general sensibilities. The unique advice in this book can radically transform your results with women, but only if you apply it.

So to begin, let's dissect the habits that you'll need to internalize.

After that, I'll offer you a challenge.

This challenge will test the limits of your comfort zone, but it will also give you a glimpse of your unseen potential in dating and in life. So I implore you to take this seriously.

Good luck.

Chapter One

YOU WILL CULTIVATE A POSITIVE STATE AND INVEST IN YOURSELF EVERY DAY

A lot of people ask me how I'm so optimistic all of the time.

The truth is, my life isn't always sunshine and unicorns. When shit hits the fan I get mad, upset and frustrated just like anyone else. However, my day-to-day emotional state is vastly different today compared to how it was a few years ago.

Instead of waking up mildly depressed and crawling out of bed after hitting the snooze button ten times, I wake up naturally with a smile on my face and motivated to kick some ass.

What changed? My morning ritual.

Your morning ritual is what sets the tone for the rest of the day.

Some people hit the snooze button a dozen times before unwillingly dragging themselves out of bed. Then they force some food down their throat, get dressed and dash off to their car or train station before their hair has even dried.

Given the choice, these people would rather sleep and wait for an external force to pull them out of bed instead of taking charge and creating their own reason to wake up.

This is a mistake.

What you do in the morning dictates how your entire day will be because it sets up your emotional state and frame of mind.

I know what you're thinking.

"Why the hell does it matter if I feel positive and emotionally centered? All I want to do is meet beautiful women."

I'll give you one simple reason:

If you stay ready, you don't have to get ready.

You don't know when you'll see your perfect ten stroll right past you. It could be at the supermarket, on the street, at a bar, but you need to feel grounded enough to go up and strike up a conversation with her. Your emotional state needs to be under your control.

Take a moment to think about what a day in the life of a beautiful single girl is like. There isn't going to be a day that goes by in which she doesn't want to meet the guy who will sweep her off her feet. That's why she puts on make-up to go to the supermarket or the gym. I had one client who met a girl who used to spend every Sunday afternoon reading in a coffee shop. Do you think she could have read somewhere else, at home or in the library? Of course, but she chose to put herself in that situation because subconsciously, on some level, she wanted to be approached.

You need to 'prime' yourself and your mindset every morning for the best possible outcome and be ready to meet women when the opportunity presents itself.

If you're in a 'reactive' state of mind from the moment you get up, you're always going to feel like things are slipping out of your control. The reason a good morning routine is so important is because you're dedicating that first bit of focus and energy to yourself. You aren't reacting to your boss's emails, watching mindless YouTube videos, or shuffling papers for that meeting you have to prepare for, but you put yourself FIRST.

You cherish yourself and improve in the process. You are a *proactive* force in your life, **NOT** a *reactive* one. You're on the attack instead of always being on the defensive.

You're going to hear me repeat that mantra a lot in the book:

"Active, not reactive."

If your default state in life is to be proactive, that means you aggressively take action and exert your will in all areas you wish to improve upon. This is the mindset of an attractive man. It's a deep internal wiring that you can also condition yourself to have. However, if your default is to react to whatever the world throws at you, your trajectory in life will be determined by the will of others. It's to play the victim instead of the hero because, when it comes down to it, the world will treat you however you let it.

Now, I know you've bought this book to improve your dating life, which tells me you want to take responsibility and become the hero of your own story, not the victim.

Bravo, you've already taken the first step.

Priming yourself for success every morning will help you cultivate a proactive mindset. You send a clear signal to yourself that you are worth investing in. You're not a victim of circumstance, but you take ownership and responsibility for any situation you get yourself into. This has huge implications in dating because it directly affects how women will perceive you. By recalibrating your internal compass, the world will acknowledge you as a man who is confident and in control of his own destiny.

If you invest in yourself every day, then you intrinsically reinforce and acknowledge your inherent value as a person. You understand the great life and future you have in front of you. You're more self-aware about your ambitious goals and understand that any woman that you meet is lucky to be dating you because they can feel you're a man on his own path in life.

On your mission to live your life to the fullest.

Now let's look at the other end of the spectrum.

Let me describe what happens when guys who don't have a great deal of success with women finally meet an attractive one. Perhaps they stumble across a beautiful woman at work, school, or out in public. She is pleasant and friendly, but not flirtatious. The guy misinterprets her demeanor as something more than it is. She may have been half-interested at first, but he constantly bugs her on social media, over WhatsApp, or by sending endless text messages.

He says too much too soon. He loses his cool and confesses his undying love for her. He buys her flowers. He dreams late at night about the incredible life and family they will have together.

She's done little more than humor the idea of letting this guy buy her a cup of coffee, and he's already planning the wedding.

Desperation and neediness are the two qualities that all women are repelled by. They come from a place of scarcity and insecurity, and a man who pursues women from this place radiates low self-esteem and lack of options – very unattractive.

I've observed thousands of interactions just like this between my clients and the women they're pursuing. Neediness simply kills all attraction. It shows that you have a lack of options and are willing to compromise your self-respect just for the chance to see her again.

Do you honestly believe a woman will want a man like this?

Even if your love life is marked by scarcity and low self-esteem, you can't let that show. And later in the book we'll talk about how to turn scarcity into abundance, and low self-esteem into deep confidence.

A high-caliber woman wants to feel like she has won you over. Women can pick up on whether you're needy, or over-eager, or compensating for something, all of which spell one thing: low confidence. And just like dogs can smell fear, women can smell your lack of confidence from a mile away.

The good news is, by setting the tone for your day with a morning routine, you'll be starting on the path to greater confidence and greater attraction.

To put it simply:

Bad morning = bad day.

Good morning = good day.

Simple, right?

The morning ritual is all about grounding your day in self-respect, investing in yourself, cultivating a proactive mindset and a powerful internal compass. It's about developing self-belief and confidence in your abilities, which is perhaps the most important thing women look for in a man.

After testing countless morning rituals over the years, I now start my day in three phases.

Phase 1:
- ☐ Smile
- ☐ Breathe deeply
- ☐ Drink lemon water and stretch

Phase 2:

(Make tea or coffee and find a quiet place to sit down first.)
- ☐ Meditate
- ☐ Gratitude journaling — write down 3 things I am grateful for.
- ☐ Connect with my vision — think about my purpose and big life goals right now.

- ❐ Visualize my day — see myself finishing my ritual, showering, getting dressed and kicking ass.

I know you might think some of this stuff is a little 'out there', like visualization or affirmations. I get the same confused look when I tell guys to meditate.

In reality, meditation is nothing more than sitting down, focusing on your breathing, calming your mind, and observing your thoughts. You can sit cross legged on the floor, in a chair with a straight back, or in any position. The point is, find someplace quiet, close your eyes, and focus on deep rhythmic breathing. That's it.

When you do this, you begin to calm your mind. You discover how to become present to the moment and enjoy each moment that your life brings.

Deliberately taking some time to introspect and investigate your inner world can be daunting at first, but this is how you replenish and nourish your mind. Someone who's spent their entire life constantly surrounded by others, avoiding being alone, will have a hard time doing this, but spending some quiet time alone in your own thoughts is how you will gain clarity of thought and true focus.

Alone time is growth time.

Not only will meditating help you focus, gain clarity, eliminate anxiety and master your own thoughts, it will make you more present.

Over time you will become more present and at ease when you spend time with other people.

Instead of compulsively checking your phone every five minutes – like everyone else does – you'll be present. Engaged. Energized. Men are biologically hard-wired to notice physical attraction first, but women? Studies have shown that women are drawn to mindfulness in men.[1]

Meditating can help with this, and it also reduces anxiety and releases a ton of 'happy hormones' in your brain like dopamine, oxytocin, and serotonin.

Start with 10 minutes of meditation each day. Personally, I like to sit with headphones and use an app like brain.fm which uses binaural beats. Some people like to use apps like Headspace or Calm, or guided meditations on YouTube. Try a few different methods until you find the best fit for you.

The next component of my morning ritual is **visualization**.

Visualization is one of your most powerful tools to help make changes in your life. The mind cannot distinguish between a thought that is remembered and one that is imagined. That is very powerful.

Imagination is the tool that has transformed the world around you. Everything around you right now is the result of an idea that someone manifested in their imagination. There have been some great studies done on the power of using your imagination to your own benefit.

---

[1] Janz, Philip, Christopher A. Pepping, and W. Kim Halford. "Individual differences in dispositional mindfulness and initial romantic attraction: A speed dating experiment." *Personality and Individual Differences* 82 (2015): 14-19.

In one study by exercise psychologist, Guang Yue,[2] weightlifters who visualized were compared to those who did not. One group trained on a regular basis. The other group was simply told to visualize their workouts instead of ever lifting a weight.

The amazing thing is that although the group that went to the gym increased their muscle mass by 30%, the visualization group increased their mass by just under half of that of the gym goers (13.5%) over a three-month period. Isn't that ridiculous? The power of visualization is real. You can change your physiology just by engaging your mental muscle and imagining.

Another scientist, Alan Richardson,[3] ran a similar experiment. His goal was to help basketball players improve their free throw. He had three groups: one group that practiced free throws on a basketball court, one that just visualized practicing and one that did nothing.

The visualizing group's improvement was just slightly below the group that actually practiced every day. The first group improved their free throws by 24% and the second by 23%.

This is why visualization is a crucial part of the morning routine, because I want you guys to visualize getting the dates, sex, lifestyle that you truly want. Just by virtue of visualizing it you will begin to attract it and create it in your life. Remember though, visualization is just the first step; you still need to get out there and do it!

There are a million different visualization techniques out there, but I find the simple approach is the most effective. Visualize yourself

---

[2] Ranganathan, Vinoth K., et al. "From mental power to muscle power—gaining strength by using the mind." *Neuropsychologia* 42.7 (2004): 944-956.
[3] http://www.llewellyn.com/encyclopedia/article/244

accomplishing your big goals in life. How do you feel? Where are you? What can you see? Who are you with? What do you look like?

Really feel what your life would be like down to every last detail, no matter how small.

Once you've done that, work your way backwards to your current life. What are the meetings you'll have today? How would today go if it was a complete success? What would you do in your dating life? Who would you meet? What news would you get? What will you be grateful for today?

Visualize your life. Visualize your year. Then visualize your month, week, and ultimately every single day.

You need to *deeply* feel yourself doing the things you visualize yourself doing.

You not only need to engage your senses of sight, hearing, touch, etc., but most importantly you need to *feel* yourself doing the things that you visualize. Whether that brings you fear, excitement, elation, it doesn't matter, but you need to anticipate what it would be like to be there and doing it in the flesh.

If you're visualizing yourself approaching that woman at the coffee shop, feel the fear, the excitement and the power that comes with it. If you're visualizing that pitch you're about to make, you need to hear your voice projecting across the room, and the reactions of the people you're trying to win over.

This is vital. Without this you're still an observer. It's like you're looking at a television; you're still separated from the experience.

Visualizing the events you want to manifest will help ensure they actual happen.

I think about my visualizations like they were memories. I look at them as if I've already accomplished them, and now I'm just retracing the steps I took to get there. Utilizing this idea is powerful because after your visualization you begin to walk, talk and act like a man that has accomplished his dreams. People, circumstances and opportunities begin to circle around you, and your visualizations become self-fulfilling prophecies.

FEED YOUR MIND WITH EMPOWERING, POSITIVE INFORMATION

So you've done your meditation and finished your visualization practice, but there's one final step before you start your day: it's time to feed your mind with positive information.

Motivational speaker Jim Rohn always said *"put in junk, out comes more junk"*.

When you clutter your mind with negativity and garbage it affects your thoughts, your ideas, and the very words that come out of your mouth. TV, news, magazines, and other media are mostly designed to put negative information into your mind.

We live in a consumer world which desperately wants to keep you in a dazed, zombie-like state of fear and anxiety with no creative ideas of your own. When you get rid of that junk and replace it with positive, empowering information from challenging books, documentaries, or podcasts, you will change from the inside out.

There's a world-renowned dance choreographer in New York City named Twyla Tharp who has a very specific process for every new production she starts working on. She's a true creative genius, and before starting on a new project she starts with an empty box. Anything that inspires her or moves her or coaxes her into forming new ideas for the project – it all goes in the box. Over time, she adds to the box, adding new layers of complexity and new sources of inspiration and ideas until, eventually, it all comes together and the result is her performance piece, a piece of art.

Now, I know you're not a dance choreographer, so you don't need a physical box if you don't want. You do, however, have a box that stores information already – your mind. Twyla fills her box with all the juicy morsels that bring her joy and spark inspiration and get her idea machine running hot. You?

What do you put in your box? What do you fill your mind with?

Do you feed it with information and knowledge and wisdom that makes you better and more positive?

Or do you feed it junk that keeps you feeling dull, complacent, unchallenged, and afraid to change?

Consciously or otherwise, you are the result of everything you put in your head – it's a form of social conditioning. If you don't fill your head with new, positive ideas, knowledge, and wisdom, you probably aren't going to be very smart, very happy, or very open to growing as a person.

Whether you know it or not, your thoughts are largely the result of the collective stimuli you *allow* into your consciousness.

You are what you eat (and I'm not talking about food).

Gandhi put it like this:

Powerful stuff.

It's the hierarchy of change that can either destroy you or make you successful.

Now, your thoughts are simply the result of the collective stimuli you're exposed to on a daily basis.

With this in mind, it's easy to see why most people are unhappy and paralyzed by fear. They've allowed mass media and social conditioning to fill their mind with junk that they've been operating on subconsciously. Becoming self-aware of the fear-based paradigms that are fed to you on a daily basis can be life-changing.

Let's look more closely at this idea of social conditioning.

Social conditioning is all around us. It's in everything you do. It's in everything you eat. It's in everything you wear. Sometimes it grabs your attention. Sometimes it's just the humdrum of your everyday existence. It never stops and it never sleeps. It is omnipresent from the moment you open your eyes to the moment you fall asleep.

Social conditioning is the basis of your mindset, psychology and self-perception. It is the collective information that feeds into your whole mental and emotional ecosystem. With this information, you feed your world view, your beliefs, and behaviors. It affects how you act and what you say.

Social conditioning can be bad, but it can also be good. We all like to think of ourselves as free thinking individuals but the reality is much different.

The majority of our social conditioning comes from mass media such as television shows, TV commercials, YouTube, the news, friends and family. Unfortunately, while there are vital beliefs and behaviors you learn from all these sources, not all of them are in your best interest. Yes, this includes your parents too.

Let me explain further. Mass media has sold you certain ideas. Ideas that benefit them a lot more than you.

For example, you're told that, if you buy a certain branded pair of jeans or sneakers suddenly you'll be 'cool' and women will desire you. You can see this very direct form of social conditioning on a daily basis. Look at the huge billboards, YouTube adverts and commercials you're inundated with. Perfectly photoshopped women fawning over a man wearing these sneakers. Even in the coffee shop I am in, I look up and I see a picture of a man and woman smiling happily wearing a set of matching hats. Our mind buys into these messages. The message here is very clear: if you buy these sneakers, you'll get a beautiful girl just like this. The media would have you believe that the new car, the chiseled abs, or the new sneakers are the foundation for attraction, but this is hardly the case.

This is an oversimplified example of how social conditioning affects you, but the point remains: building attraction and self-confidence cannot be bought. Adding more things to your life will not build lasting self-esteem.

Mass media targets the everyday person and tries to make you believe you are insecure, uncool and frightened so that you purchase what they want. It's the reason why you're told you need a six pack or the latest trendy clothes to fit in. Most of us foolishly buy into all of this and 'do as we're told'.

We spend frivolously to try to cover up our insecurities. This creates what I call group think and peer pressure. You no longer give yourself permission for what to wear, think or feel. You look around and just copy those people you deem 'cool'. You go to bars and parties and spend money on drinks to fit in because that's what you're supposed to be doing. You don't approach a woman during the day because no one else is giving you permission to do so. You go to a job you hate because you feel like the job market is 'risky' and you could end up on the street if you set out to find another form of meaningful employment.

These are all socially conditioned ideas and fear-based paradigms.

Social conditioning isn't just about making money from consumers though. The other part of social conditioning is less direct and can have just as bad if not worse implications for you.

Depending on how lucky or unlucky you are.

We now know that we model ourselves on the information we're fed, and even the information we choose. From an early age, we have been modeling our behaviors, beliefs and social skills on our parents and friends. If you had great parents who instilled in you high self-esteem and confidence, perhaps they challenged you, encouraged you to develop mental fortitude in times of difficulty and even advised you through the tricky realm of sexual and dating relationships.

Congratulations.

You should call your parents right now and tell them how grateful you are for them.

The majority of parents do love their children but unfortunately pass down some of their insecurities, negativity, and bad habits. And if parents had an unhealthy, strained relationship, we subconsciously model some of their beliefs and value systems. Now, before I carry on I don't want you to go away and start blaming your parents. Most parents do the best they can. They're only human after all, and nobody's perfect. If you blame others you're shirking responsibility. You're playing the victim. Instead, take ownership of your life and take action to correct it. You are responsible for your life so start putting in the work to change it.

It's not just your parents you learned from. It's your peers in schools, your acquaintances at the gym or in your men's club. In fact, one of the most prominent places in which you are being conditioned at this moment is your current friendship circle.

There's this famous self-development quote:

"You are the product of the five people you spend the most time with."

To take this one step further:

"You are the result of everything you allow into your life and your consciousness."

Luckily for you, all of this is within your control. You choose who you spend your time with and how you spend it. Hopefully you'll pick more carefully moving forward, and surround yourself with people and information that encourage you to become better, smarter, and stronger.

I hope I am awakening you. And that you begin to realize a lot of your insecurities are fabricated. A lot of your struggles in dating are a result of you modeling Hollywood movies and advertisements, thinking that if you replicate what they suggest, you will get a similar result in your life. Some of your bad behaviors may have even been learnt through looking at friends and family members and modeling their relationship strategies.

That's the bad news. However, there is some **good news.**

There are two strategies to help you overcome this.

The first is awareness, which you've now cultivated. From today onwards apply this to the myriad messages and influences vying for your attention and seeping into your consciousness. You will curate the information you internalize and discard anything that does not make you better.

The second strategy is reprogramming your mind.

I've found that the most effective way to reprogram your mind to be happy, confident, and positive all the time is to feed it with good information and correct the social conditioning that has been making growth and success impossible. Give yourself permission to do things that you want to do no matter what other people are doing around you.

For example, if you do see a beautiful woman walking down the street go up to her. You'll see guys checking her out but they will not engage her. Why? Because they are stuck in their heads, in their own socially conditioned narrative.

Start making decisions based on your own internal thoughts and feelings. *Be internally referenced.*

This doesn't just go for striking up conversations with women, it goes for things like starting a business even if it contradicts what friends and colleagues may express about it. It means revamping your diet when everyone in your family has traditionally eaten unhealthily. It means going against the grain, if necessary, to better yourself and your life.

Give yourself permission to do what you want in your life.

Give yourself permission to improve and learn. Committing to as little as twenty minutes each morning of reading or listening to an audiobook can have noticeable results.

Do you have to include all of these things into your morning ritual?

Absolutely not, you should start with what you can comfortably manage each day. The key is replacing a disempowering morning ritual with an empowering one. At the very least start with meditation and reading every single day.

Feel free to find a combination of practices that work for you, but for me this entire process takes less than 45 minutes:

- ❒ Smile
- ❒ Breathe deeply
- ❒ Drink water and stretch

- ☐ Meditate
- ☐ Gratitude — think of 3 things I am grateful for
- ☐ Connect with my vision — think about my purpose and goals
- ☐ Visualize my day — see myself finishing my ritual, showering, getting dressed and kicking ass
- ☐ Read

HARSH TRUTH

You may feel like you don't have that 45 minutes to spare. It doesn't even need to take that long, but let's hypothetically say it does. How do you create more time for yourself?

Simple. Wake up EARLIER.

There are only so many hours in the day and waking up early allows you to start getting things done while the rest of the world is still asleep. It gives you a competitive edge over others, and the morning time is the most productive time. Human beings are biologically designed to wake up with the sun.

Modern day society has ruined us with artificial lighting and blue-light-emitting screens that have wreaked havoc on our sleep-wake cycles and circadian rhythms.

The solution is very simple, wake up how nature intended (early) and feel GOOD about yourself.

Now, no matter what your morning ritual is, you can't have a good day if you are waking up after 12pm. By waking up late you are missing out on the most productive time of day.

Accomplishing this is easier than you think.

- ❒ Before midnight, turn off all screens — artificial lighting will impair melatonin production (the sleep hormone) from your pineal gland.
- ❒ Develop a night-time ritual where you shut off your brain at least 1 hour before bed, read some fiction or drink tea and meditate.
- ❒ Black out blinds, ear plugs and an expensive mattress will all help you get to sleep before midnight.

So, you better start taking advantage of your time and making every single day count.

If you are waking up early already are you honestly telling me, you don't have 45 minutes to focus on yourself?

If you feel like you need more time to sleep then go to bed earlier. This metamorphosis is not about making excuses. If you want the results you need to find a solution instead of always looking for the problems or reasons you can't do something.

One more bonus tip: turn your phone to airplane mode before you sleep and don't turn it back on until your morning routine is done. The temptation to check social media and your emails first thing in the morning will be too high, and let me tell you, it's a fast track to throwing off your entire day. Don't do it.

ACTION STEPS

1. Further reading: *The Presence Process* by Michael Brown.
2. Look at your social circle of friends and decide if you are part of a group that empowers you or brings you down.
3. Actively think about everything you watch, read, listen to – any incoming information at all – and ask yourself these questions: What am I learning here? Is this making me feel positive or negative? Is this useful? Can this help me solve my problems or reach my goals?
4. Start giving yourself permission to do things that you've always wanted to in your life. Think about what things you've held back because of social conditioning or fear of judgment of those around you.
5. I highly recommend checking out the Five Minute Journal. If you struggle with committing to writing down what you accomplish or are grateful each day this beautifully crafted journal can sit on your bedside table so you don't forget. I don't have an affiliation with the makers of the journal, I just genuinely believe it to be a great tool to better yourself.
6. Write down 3 – 5 goals for the next year. If you're struggling to visualize the life or even the kind of woman you want to attract into your life maybe you need to define for yourself what those look like. We have several classes and videos on writing goals and visualization on our YouTube channel. So, we can walk you through that process step by step.
7. Grab our official Attraction Decoded Poster – at michaelvalmont.com/30-day-challenge-poster and you can

put this on your wall to aid you with your morning routine and daily habits.

Chapter Two

YOU WILL TACKLE FEAR AND ANXIETY HEAD ON

Heroes are gods. They are worshipped by men and fawned over by women.

We look up to characters like Achilles marching on the beaches of Troy or James Bond seducing beautiful women while foiling plots by evil forces …all in spectacular style. Consider someone like Steve Jobs, who was fired from Apple and not only came back as the CEO but revolutionized the computing and mobile phone industry. Or Nelson Mandela, who spent 27 years in prison in South Africa because he would not back down on his beliefs. Unbreakable spirit.

Those are some examples of men who, in the face of great adversity, challenge and fear, showed tremendous courage.

In this chapter I will shine a light on fear and teach you how to create the habit of taking action in spite of that fear.

A key thing to realize is that you must be the hero of your own story. There is *no one* coming to save you from all your fears and anxieties that you have in your life. Let me repeat that:

No one is coming to save you.

The responsibility lies with you. Others can help, but it is you who must act in the face of fear to get what you want from life.

The corollary to the 'hero of your own story' is this idea of fearlessness. There's this idea that the heroes we admire are never afraid.

That is complete nonsense.

Heroes feel fear just the same as you do. The idea isn't to eliminate fear altogether but to learn from it and act in spite of the fear.

That's why they're heroes, because they feel the fear and take action anyway.

I was watching a documentary about Mike Tyson several years ago and in the film, Tyson's trainer, Cus D'Amato, said something that really resonated with me:

"The hero and the coward both feel the same thing, but the hero uses his fear while the coward runs. It's the same thing, fear, but it's what you do with it that matters".

It was in this moment I realized that the goal is not to eliminate fear, no. It was not about wishing away fear, pretending it did not exist or burying it deep within.

It was about accepting the fear, acknowledging it and acting anyway. There is a great book called Feel The Fear and Do It Anyway by Susan Jeffers, which talks at length about this.

Another idea that has served my clients and me is this idea of "attacking" your fears. Instead of avoiding the things that you are afraid of, you confront them. You take the offensive, get aggressive, and use the fear to show you what you need to do next.

On my courses and programs, I teach guys to frame their fears as their true north compass.

In most cases, the thing you're trying to avoid is precisely what you need to confront.

Use your fear to point you in the direction of the places in your life that have the greatest opportunity for growth. Sometimes that can mean taking the first step towards accomplishing your dreams and aspirations.

If you see that gorgeous girl walking down the street, start a conversation with her. You want to challenge your boss in the meeting, do it. Scared of starting a business because that's what you've always wanted? Face the fear and get started.

You build confidence by following your true north compass on a daily basis, and steadily working to turn those fears into strengths.

A lot of people assume confidence is something you're born with, but in reality confidence is almost entirely the result of putting in the effort and the work to become proficient at something – usually this means a skill. I put in the reps to become very competent at attracting women, therefore I am confident enough to share my ideas and experiences in this book to help others succeed.

I put in the reps, built that muscle – that confidence – and now it's simply one skill among many that I've cultivated.

Fear of the unknown gives us anxiety. It's why a lot of children are scared of the dark, because you can't see what hides behind the black curtain of darkness. By putting in the reps, leaning into this fear, and learning from your mistakes, over time you will develop competence in anything you want. In most cases, you can substitute out confidence for one word: skill. As you slowly develop competency at a skill (like interacting with women), you become more confident because you know the strength of your own abilities.

Simply put, **competence builds confidence.**

Why are women attracted to guys who have great social networks, play recreational sports with their friends, or play in a band? Having a great social network is a signal that you'll be a fun, social person who is great with people – it shows that you have competent social skills. Playing sports signals that you're healthy, in shape, and like to stay active. Playing an instrument shows you can set your mind to learning something new and follow through – it shows persistence, competence, and creativity. Granted, those are three examples out of a million, but the point is clear: being proactive and DOING things – and doing them well – is eminently attractive to women. As Joe Rogan crudely put it in one of his recent podcasts:

> "Focus on being an excellent person and women will want to fuck you".
> **JOE ROGAN**

I approach most activities from a place of confidence because I've put in the time to get good at them, but there are some areas that I wouldn't necessarily flourish. For example, I have a terrible singing voice. I don't mind rocking the Karaoke, but you won't find me auditioning for American Idol anytime soon. Not because I lack core confidence, but because singing is just something I do for fun, not because I'm good at it. It's not a skill I care to develop.

Living your life by the 'active, not reactive' mantra means attacking your fears.

Fear shouldn't be something you deal with by hiding in the shadows and only confronting it when you're left with no choice, but should be handled by picking up your sword every single day and slaying your demons. It is a deliberate choice that cultivates huge internal strength.

So why are we afraid of the things we want anyway?

Anyone who has a basic knowledge of biology realizes that our brains have evolved into extraordinary supercomputers. They allow us to plan, to visualize, to calculate, to imagine, and to build a world around us that has drastically transformed over the past decade.

As amazing as our brains are, some of the programming is outdated.

Yes, I am saying that the external world has moved so fast that our biology has been unable to catch up in some respects. What we once needed to be afraid of is no longer important to our survival, yet our body still responds defensively.

You go to stand at the edge of a very tall building. Suddenly you feel woozy and lightheaded. Your body screams at you to move away because it thinks you are in grave danger. However, you know the truth. There is a railing separating you from death and protecting you. So why is your body acting so afraid?

We live in a world of outdated evolutionary biology.

Thousands of years ago there was no railing. You would be in danger if you moved towards the face of a big cliff.

It's for that same reason, when you see that woman and you want to go up to her, you hesitate. You know on a logical level that there would be no physical consequences of speaking to her, but that crippling biological fear prevents you from immediately engaging her in conversation.

I've had grizzled war veterans, special forces, and armed militia shaking at the knees when they see attractive women they want to approach. I've literally coached people whose job was to hunt wolves who had been stalking and eating children and even THEY were terrified of starting up conversations with women. These are men that had to face DEATH on a daily basis.

So how could they possibly be afraid of talking to a lovely woman?

There are a multitude of reasons. Fear of rejection. Fear of failure. But the key reason these people are afraid is a hard-wired biological trigger. Our biology still believes that our safety might be threatened if we go up to a woman and start a conversation with her. Tens of thousands of years ago we existed in tribes and if you went up to the wrong woman you actually *could* be in physical danger, just like in the cliff example.

Competing for women has always been about status but, back then, if you went up to the most attractive woman in the tribe, a confrontation with a competing alpha male could easily mean being bashed over the head with a club. Even if it did not result in death, your physical and social isolation from a tribe would leave you to fend for yourself, which would usually result in death anyway. You also have to remember that population size was not 7 billion people globally like it is now. In fact, if we go back just 2000 years our estimated population size was at just 200-300 million globally. Tribes were still large but more physically separated. In today's culture we have mega-cities and even if you are in a small village, it's not hard to get up and relocate.[4]

That's the reason why your brain short circuits when you see that gorgeous girl; unless you're drunk – which might help you initiate conversation, but completely destroys your chances of authentically connecting with her.

So, when you walk up to a woman, your evolved, pre-frontal cortex says: "It's ok, there are no consequences of going up to her. Who cares what anyone else thinks if they see me? Or who cares what she thinks of me?"

But the other part, your prehistoric lizard brain says: "Don't do it, you'll be in danger." That's the conflict.

That's why you walk away, stew on your failure to engage, and beat yourself up.

---

[4] McDonald, Melissa M., Carlos David Navarrete, and Mark Van Vugt. "Evolution and the psychology of intergroup conflict: The male warrior hypothesis." Phil. Trans. R. Soc. B 367.1589 (2012): 670-679.

So what's the solution?

There's a saying in Jiu Jitsu that goes like this:

"In Jiu Jitsu there is no failing, only learning."

When building any skill, you're probably going to fail – A LOT – but if you pay attention, you'll learn what went wrong and how you can improve next time.

That's what learning is!

I used to be awful with women, but over the course of years of trial and error and leaning into those fears, I got better. And after that I kept improving even more.

It's just like working out.

Most people start working out to get in shape, but once they see even the smallest improvement, they become obsessed with getting even better. It becomes an addiction. That's how you should approach overcoming your fears. Make fear your best friend and use it as a signal to take action and to learn from, not as something to rule your life and hold you back.

The great thing about facing your fears is that it's a skill and, like any skill, it can be learned.

The fear might have been warranted back then, but unlike our prehistoric ancestors, you won't die if you approach a woman in modern society.

The only catch is you have to take that first step and face the fear.

Your fight or flight response may go off. Your adrenaline might get pumping, your palms might get sweaty, but no matter what happens during that initial encounter, you can learn from the experience and do better next time.

Your brain is a master of learning about when to induce the anxiety and hyper-alert fight or flight response. The limbic system in the brain learns which situations you correctly need a heightened adrenaline and cortisone response to.

Some people learn from an embarrassing first rejection by a girl in their past: their limbic system learns to activate when in a situation with an attractive girl otherwise they may be humiliated and socially exposed. Some men's limbic system sits dormant when they are engaging a beautiful woman. Why? Because their first experience was positive or non-threatening.

I liken this to the first time you did a math equation.

The first time you did a math equation, you usually had one of two responses: you were either a "natural" and it pretty much clicked on your first shot. Or you couldn't do it, gave up and declared "math just isn't for me." You then avoid math, and your seemingly innate lack of mathematical skill becomes a self-fulfilling prophecy.

It's the same thing with getting rejected by a beautiful woman. The limbic system in the brain can learn at any point in your life, and it can learn that you shouldn't be afraid of beautiful women when you go up to them. Your anxiety disintegrates, piece by piece, to the point that you're in complete control when you engage a beautiful woman. Guys that are 'naturally' good with women have these experiences early on and become very at ease around beautiful women from a young age. You can achieve the same level of success with women by putting yourself through a similar process.

The key point to keep in mind is that while you may be terrified of engaging and approaching women for the first several times, you will survive. Unlike our prehistoric ancestors, nobody is coming to bash you with a club. Once you realize that, then you can focus on cultivating the skills of attraction.

It's all about taking that first step. Then the next. And the next.

You need to persistently and regularly challenge fear in dating and all areas of your life. Only then can you learn how to feel the fear, but take action anyway.

I have a powerful framing technique I use to approach women called "assuming familiarity and attraction."

This means that you assume that she is attracted to you. Your underlying basis is that everything she does is as a result of her attraction for you. You engage her like you know this is true already. Assume that you already know her, like she's an old friend that you haven't spoken to in a few years. This will eradicate that terrible fear of judgment that you have. "I know her well, what's the big deal?" is the mentality that you have.

The reality is that whatever message or feelings you project, she will mirror back to you. So, by assuming attraction it can become a self-fulfilling prophecy. When you're starting conversations with beautiful women there isn't anything magical you need to do; no special conversational skills or anything else you may have heard or read.

So what are the key habits and pieces of action that I want you to take based off our new-found understanding of fear?

ACTION STEPS

- ☐ Do one thing that scares you every day, no matter how small.
- ☐ Engage three new women a day, making sure you are genuinely attracted to them, stone cold sober for at least one month (more on this later).
- ☐ Use fear as a daily compass to guide your attention and action.
- ☐ Initiate conversations with beautiful women and assume attraction.
- ☐ Write down a list of things that scare you and work to engage with those fears on a regular basis.
- ☐ Create accountability; at the end of every day, if you feel like there was something you didn't do because you were scared, write it on a sticky note and put it on your wall or dressing mirror. The next morning take it off and bring it with you and correct that 'mistake'. This is a great tool for slowly building self-esteem over time.

Chapter Three

YOU WILL LOOK AND FEEL YOUR BEST EVERY DAY

'Dress for success', remember that one?

That's right.

I am stating that physical appearance matters.

In fact, it matters a lot when it comes to attracting women and making a great first impression.

Can you become successful looking like a slob every day? Of course you can, if you have other stellar attributes like massive status, wealth, or charisma, but improving your physical appearance is the best 'quick fix' for regular guys who want to do better with women.

I'm not saying you need to obsess over your physical appearance. In fact, **don't** do this. Some guys drop all the other important personal development work just to obsess over their reflection in the mirror.

Making sure you're not visually repulsive to women is important because it signals what you think about yourself.

With just a few adjustments to your appearance, you can almost instantly transform yourself from average to awesome, both in terms of how you look and how you feel. If you consistently make an effort to improve your appearance, you can't help but feel more confident, and people will start to notice.

I recently had one client show up to a coaching session who wanted to talk to me about how awful his dating life was. Before he even opened his mouth, I knew exactly what his problem was. I think he was working with the same wardrobe he had when he was a 12-year-old.

He looked like the real-life, grown-up version of Bart Simpson.

Dressing poorly communicates lack of self-awareness and lack of effort.

Looking like our man-boy Bart Simpson from above isn't sexy, and neither is looking like a slob. You will instantly be judged by your outward appearance – this is human nature. It is fact. This includes your weight, skin complexion, grooming, body shape, and clothes.

I understand that there is a superficial nature to what I'm saying. I wish it wasn't this way. But if you aren't grooming yourself women will be repulsed by you, so get used to putting some effort into it.

Image is only one piece of the self-development puzzle. Your self-perception, self-image and self-esteem work are all more important than your clothing. However, if we're looking at maximizing your results we want to change both the internal and the external too.

I always say if you can change a shirt and get 10% better results, it's worth it.

This chapter isn't just about the shirt you wear, though. It's about your body's biochemistry. It's about your energy levels, your testosterone and mental clarity.

Here are some of the best things you can do today to feel better about yourself and become more attractive to women.

START WORKING OUT

If you're a single guy under the age of 50 there is absolutely no excuse for not working out.

You can't look good if you're in poor shape and poorly groomed, no matter what clothes you buy. The solution is simple, join a gym and go at least 3 times a week. We're looking for the 1% daily improvement in your health and in everything you do. We're looking at the long-term results; this is the diametric opposite to the 'magic pill' or instant result you may desire. Our old friend social conditioning may say you can have it quick and easy but it's simply not the case.

Working out, just like making the effort in your appearance, communicates that you have self-respect. It also makes you feel more confident. It makes you feel strong and powerful. Like a Spartan warrior. It activates genes within you that are the result of thousands of years of evolution. Men are meant to feel strong and to lead; it is literally wired into our DNA. Hence why we produce much more testosterone than women. Use it. That way, when you do meet that girl, you can lift her up. Show her your strength. That makes you feel like a man and makes her feel like a woman. She'll love that.

There are all kinds of ways to get in shape. My favorite for a lot of guys is lifting weights. Sticking to a diet of compound lifts like the squat, deadlift, bench press, pull-ups, and push-ups will be enough to progress on for years. Those are fundamental lifts that work the most muscle groups and will get you strong and fit. You should consult some bodybuilding or fitness expert for more information on this.

A lot of guys think they need to achieve the yoked bodybuilder or fitness model physique. This is simply not the case. Women just want to know you take care of yourself. Some of the body images perpetuated by men's fitness magazines are simply unobtainable without using steroids and growth hormones.

Some guys spend all their time working out and obsessing over their image. They are pretty insecure. Remember what we said about social conditioning? Some guys equate having a Mr. Olympian figure to being able to attract women. Finally, when they get to what they perceive to be the perfect body, their bubble is popped when they have little to no more success than they did in their 'average' body.

Instead of working out to improve themselves and to build their self-esteem and health, they do it for other people. They spend every shred of energy trying to look like the guy on the cover of Men's Health because they believe it is the sole factor for attracting women. Whilst it is important to push towards your fitness and body goals for the reasons I mentioned above… *Do not be fooled into replacing one insecurity with another.*

Developing a physique in the top 0.001% is great for those who have careers in health and fitness, but for the majority of guys this is not an effective way to spend your time unless it is coming from a healthy place of passion and not fear.

Women can smell this overcompensation from a mile away. If you're strong and active in some form or another and your chest is bigger than your gut, you're already ahead of most guys.

Do not use this as an excuse to avoid working out or to be undisciplined in your diet. This is about becoming the best that you can be and only you can measure the true effort you're putting into changing.

Another great way to get in shape and stay active is to practice a combative martial art like Brazilian Jiu Jitsu, boxing or Thai boxing. Nothing wakes up your testosterone or innate primal instincts like combative situations. There is something very raw and primal about engaging in physical combat. Learning how to exert your will and defend yourself in combat is a huge way to build confidence that you can take with you from the gym and out into the world.

CHANGE YOUR DIET

Diet plays a massive role not only in how you feel but on your overall appearance and sex drive. Cutting down on unhealthy foods will help you lose fat, look more muscular, and reconfigure your body shape, but it has even more powerful benefits that will ripple into your social and professional life.

In fact, there is a lot of new science that shows anxiety, poor attention spans and even confidence are drastically affected by your diet. Just think about the implication of this for a second.

Imagine the depression, anxiety and concentration issues that you may have experienced are a result of the diet and food you consume. It may be that with the correct nutrition, supplementation, and vitamin intake you can completely counteract those psychological issues. One comprehensive nutritional study looks at the link between mental health disorders and nutrition that so many doctors and health practitioners fail to make.

"Studies have indicated that daily supplements of vital nutrients are often effective in reducing patients' symptoms. Supplements containing amino acids have also been found to reduce symptoms, as they are converted to neurotransmitters which in turn alleviate depression and other mental health problems. On the basis of accumulating scientific evidence, an effective therapeutic intervention is emerging, namely nutritional supplement/treatment. These may be appropriate for controlling and to some extent, preventing depression, bipolar disorder, schizophrenia, eating disorders and anxiety disorders, attention deficit disorder/attention deficit hyperactivity disorder (ADD/ADHD), autism, and addiction."[5]

The consequences of such a study for you are huge. This means that some of your negativity and anxiety may actually be worsened or even created by the food you are eating!

---

5   Rao, TS Sathyanarayana, et al. "Understanding nutrition, depression and mental illnesses." *Indian journal of psychiatry* 50.2 (2008): 77.

You're constantly blaming your bad parenting or 'bad genes' for your anxiety and depression when in reality it could just be the food you eat.

So, if you're consuming a lot of junk food and alcohol, your clarity of thought will be a lot lower than someone who eats clean and drinks water.

In today's competitive world, it's like tying your shoelaces together and trying to run a marathon.

Why would you shortcut your success like that?

Your current energy level is your baseline so it feels normal, but when you change your diet, your new normal will entail less mental fog, less anxiety, more clarity, and more energy.

Also, smell. When you change your diet, you smell better.

The right diet will also improve your complexion. If you have acne problems, the odds are you're dealing with an internal problem like a food sensitivity or imbalanced gut bacteria.

If you're wondering why your acne isn't going away after applying Clearasil, yet your diet is full of unhealthy food, then you're probably not addressing the root cause of the issue.

Like most problems in life, you shouldn't be persuaded by the quick-fix options. Look for one that addresses the root of the problem, not something that simply masks the symptoms.

Acne, for example. This highlights a fundamental problem with the way doctors look at our bodies now.

Instead of looking at the system as a whole, they occupy specialized fields in medicine, such as skin, heart, liver, etc.

So if you have acne, the doctor might prescribe a cream or ointment to address the surface-level symptoms, without delving deeper into the root of the condition. Two people can have spots or a rash and have completely different underlying symptoms. One might benefit from nothing more than the cream, but another person might have something more insidious like a food allergy.

This is one of the reasons I'm fond of the holistic approach and it's something that coalesces with my dating philosophy as well: tackling the person as a whole, not trying to mask the symptoms with ineffective tricks or gimmicks.

I'm not a nutritionist or a doctor, so you must put time into doing your own research. If you're interested in further reading, I would recommend *The Ultra Mind Solution* by Dr. Mark Hyman as a starting point. His nutritional recommendations cater to the individual based on their unique needs and preferences. I would also recommend you look into the article I cited on the page above.

The fact is, no single diet is right for everyone. You have completely different genetics and DNA than me. You have different activity levels. You live in a different climate and environment than me. Therefore, we each have our own unique nutritional needs. There are some universal truths when it comes to diet, but it's also important to experiment and dig deeper into your personal nutritional needs.

For example: there are a lot of foods prevalent in the bodybuilding world that are good for building muscle but are packed with additives, sweeteners, and might not have good long-term effects on your system.

Things like processed foods, excess sugar, and soft drinks, on the other hand, should be minimized in everyone's diet. Generally speaking, the less processed it is (i.e. additives, chemicals, preservatives, refined ingredients) the better for you it will be. As the great philosopher Hippocrates said:

"Let Food Be Thy Medicine."

Food is the key. It really is. Diet is one of the best, most practical places to start if you want to radically transform your life and your health. It's the best insurance package money can buy. You can remove toxins, micro-allergens and problematic nutrients, whilst replenishing lacking minerals, healthful nutrients, and antioxidants in your body. Change your diet and watch yourself transform in a matter of weeks.

When you start eating healthy, your taste buds will literally change to crave healthy, clean food. Your body fat will drop. Your acne will clear up. Your energy will up. Mental fog gone.

You will feel healthier, more energetic, and have a greater sex drive when you eat a broad spectrum of healthy foods.

Combine that with quitting porn, working out, and some of the other cornerstone habits and it's easy to see why you'll start to feel happier and more confident.

GROOMING AND STYLE

The biggest mistake guys make in their appearance is that they don't buy clothes that fit them well.

On one side of the coin you have guys who wear the ultra-baggy, three-sizes-too-big look. You can go ahead and wear them, but we're no longer in the 90s, and you're not Snoop Dogg, so either abandon the look or find a time machine.

On the other end of the spectrum are the guys who wear clothes that are way too small, trying to show off their physique. That's not always a bad thing, unless it looks like you're wearing clothes from the kids' department. I see this all the time. If your pants don't touch the tops of your shoes, it's probably time to go clothes shopping.

For starters, find a quality shirt that fits your body type and matches your aesthetic, a nice pair of formal shoes, a well-fitting pair of jeans. If you are in any doubt about the fit, get a second opinion. Then get a third.

Dressing well doesn't have to be expensive either. Yet I see countless guys at networking sessions, at bars, and arriving for interviews who show up in a sloppy state. Now, I'm not advocating dressing up in a button-up and blazer everywhere you go, but you should take pride in your appearance because you never know when you'll have an opportunity to make a good impression.

Dressing well isn't just about women. Studies have shown that wearing nicer clothes impacts your confidence in work and business situations. For example, you're in a business meeting in a fitted suit. The stakeholders in the meeting engage you more and are more receptive to your ideas because of the way you're dressed and the way you present yourself. As you subconsciously pick up on their cues this increases your confidence and your authority and this reinforces those attributes. This is not anecdotal either, this is scientifically proven.[6]

A good rule of thumb is to wear what matches your style and aesthetic, but make sure to pick clothes that fit and are made from high-quality material, because women notice this.

Furthermore, realize that there is a difference between style and fashion. Style is timeless and fashion is based on current trends. Something that is stylish is never out of fashion, something that is fashionable is sure to be out of fashion within the next several months. You can look at someone like a Mick Jagger, Steve McQueen or Marlon Brando in 100 years' time and still be envious of their taste in clothes.

Then you can look at the mullet or the XXL jeans we talked about earlier and understand that at one time these were fashionable. Anyone with a mullet haircut or pair of JNCOs now is just a joke (no offense to my mullet and JNCO-wearing readers out there, but seriously, sort it out).

If you're looking to build a wardrobe of clothes that suits you, start by filling your wardrobe with classic style pieces. Items you can wear that are an investment that you can still wear in 10 years' time and still attract compliments.

---

6   https://www.wsj.com/articles/why-dressing-for-success-leads-to-success-1456110340

The core items I would recommend a guy having in his closet are:

- ☐ Tailored shirt
- ☐ Tailored sports jacket or blazer
- ☐ Brown leather belt
- ☐ Brown or black brogues, loafers, or classic lace-up shoes
- ☐ Fitted jeans (not an oversized factory cut)
- ☐ A nice timepiece, i.e. watch
- ☐ Classic trainers such as low-cut Converse or Vans for more casual looks
- ☐ Dark pea coat or trench coat for winter
- ☐ Plain, v-neck t-shirts

If you need further guidance on what being well-dressed means, the best resources for inspiration and ideas come from GQ.com and Fashionbeans.com. Both websites are tailored to bringing you the best in fashion and style. If you need further inspiration you could even draw it from well-dressed actors or celebrities. Remember though, avoid obnoxious logos and go for classic, timeless pieces of clothing, because those will never go out of style.

If you combine colors that suit you with well-fitted and classic pieces, and add in a sprinkle of your own personal flair, you're going to be on to a winner. Hone your own personal style and you will be making a big impact wherever you go.

SOME OTHER QUICK STYLE TIPS:

1. Represent your personality through the clothes you wear.
2. Choose clothes that make you feel comfortable. There may be an adjustment period in new, better-fitted clothing, so experiment and be patient.
3. Match the shoes and belt.
4. Try clothes on and make sure you have the right fit for your body type (not too baggy, not too tight). Ask a stylist if you're not sure.
5. If you don't know fashion, get someone to help you – perhaps a stylist, an external style consultant, or a friend with good taste. (If you've started implementing the strategies from this book, you might even have some new female friends who can help).
6. Experiment with colors. Different colors match well with different hair and skin tones. Everyone is different so to maximize your own look, be inquisitive and experimental.
7. Choose a haircut that complements your face shape. Go to an expensive salon and get their recommendation on what would suit you.
8. Experiment with facial hair. Clean shaven. Designer stubble. Medium beard. Long beard. Whatever it is, keep it neat.

The idea of 'staying ready' isn't just about grooming and appearance. It says something about who you are. It signals what you think of yourself. If you were to bump into the investor that you need for your new business idea, would your appearance communicate confidence and self-respect and make the best possible impression?

If the girl of your dreams crossed your path on your way to work would your style and self-grooming help or hinder the likelihood of getting her number?

Remember: your appearance is a direct representation of what you think about. Putting some thought into the way you look and dress will put you in the best possible position to seize any opportunity that comes your way.

ACTION STEPS:

- ☐ Eat clean and remove unhealthy processed foods from your diet.
- ☐ Implement the 8 style tips from above and study how much better people will perceive you (make sure to ask professionals for their advice on what looks best on you).
- ☐ Start doing some form of physical exercise 3x per week. Join a gym, take MMA classes, anything to get you moving.

Chapter Four

YOU WILL FOCUS ON YOUR ULTIMATE VISION AND BE PURPOSEFUL

Winners have goals in life.

They set goals, take action, measure their results and adjust course until they win.

But, what does it mean to have purpose or vision?

It means you need to be focusing on what you're passionate about in life. This does not necessarily mean that you have to be doing that for a living (though that would be ideal), but it does mean dedicating yourself to something that matters to you on a deep level.

You need to have passions that you can talk about expressively, and the only way you can do that is by having true love for an activity in your life. A lot of people resign themselves to jobs they hate. They feel stuck and do nothing to change their situation.

People like this are instinctively judged by others by the way they talk about their work. If you tell me you hate your job, the first question I would ask you is:

"Ok, well, why do you keep doing your job if you hate it?"

There is no way to answer this without making an excuse.

An excuse for not taking action to change your circumstances and pave your own path forward.

There is nothing more attractive to women than a guy who is on his path. You could clean toilets for a living, but if your work is fueled or connected with your zeal for life, if you take great pride in what you do, that'll come through in the way you speak about it.

The fact is, a man who is decisive and purposeful in his actions is infinitely more attractive than someone who makes excuses and fails to change his reality.

Masculine and feminine energy are like magnetic forces – they simply pull towards each other.

The easiest way to see this is to imagine the yin and yang.

When it comes to attracting the opposite sex, we don't attract what we want, we attract what we are. The energy you put out in the world is the same energy that will come back to you in other people. Whoever resonates with the presence you put out is what you get.

I have a deep belief in the idea of masculine energy and feminine energy; both being complementary parts of a whole system. Cultivating stronger masculinity through these traits will allow your most attractive self to shine. If you truly apply yourself to your highest purpose and gift, you will no longer need to be on the draining hamster wheel of dating. Women will proactively chase you for affection, sex and relationships. Women will sense a man on his purpose, putting time and focus into his greater goals in life and be deeply satisfied to be in a relationship with him.

One of the core masculine traits is decisiveness and a sense of purpose, and it happens to be one of the most attractive qualities women look for.

One of the best early indicators of whether it's going to work out with a guy is how the logistics are planned on the first date. If you're a decision maker, you will pick the venue, the time, and the date. Women go through all the trouble of making themselves sexy for you. They get their hair done, shave their legs, apply make-up, etc., so the least you can do is take care of the logistics.

Remember this: women want to follow your lead. They want to feel like you are in control and in charge of the situation. They want to be swept off their feet!

One of the worst things you can do when planning a first date is to ask her to make any decisions whatsoever. The more decisions you force her to make, the less she will think of you. It's that simple.

Quick, bold decision-making skills = highly attractive

Wavering, uncertain, indecision = highly unattractive

I know this because once I started owning my decisions and wearing my purpose on my sleeve, my results with women transformed. There is both a short-term shift and a long-term shift that needs to happen.

The short-term shift simply means building your decision-making muscle. Pick the venue. Tell her when you're picking her up, don't ask. If something doesn't work for her, she'll tell you, but otherwise, take control.

If you don't lead, she can't follow.

At every opportunity in your life, no matter how small or trivial it may seem, you must cultivate a doer's attitude and strive to become a decisive man of action, whether that is deciding to leave that awful job you hate or choosing the venue for your date tonight. It is about being decisive and taking the lead. It's about making decisions and owning those decisions.

I used to be so indecisive it hurt. I would go out with my friends and they would ask me:

"What movie do you want to watch?"

"Whatever, you choose."

"Where do you feel like going to dinner?"

"Whatever man, I'm easy."

Every conversation, whether with guys or with women sounded like that: it was the flimsy attitude of someone who did not value his time.

Time is our most precious commodity, and purposeful men do not let others decide how they will spend it. Being the decision maker is an act of leadership. It's to take charge, plan the course of action, and make things happen according to your will.

Now I lead in every aspect of my life and implore you to take control of your life too.

Becoming a decision maker is something you can do today – don't dawdle. Once you become a master of making the small decisions, you'll be in a better position to navigate the big decisions like quitting your job. Or starting a business. Once that decision-making muscle grows stronger, you'll be able to challenge it with bigger decisions; decisions that could change your life, not just what you'll have for dinner.

When your default is to take action and make the decisions, you will naturally feel more confident and masculine, and you will find that women are very receptive to this.

They will feel that you are living a purposeful life, not simply going through the motions of your day-to-day existence.

You see, purpose in a practical sense is about understanding your identity, values and surroundings and putting in effort to improve in one or many areas of your life. It's about knowing yourself, your strengths and weaknesses down to your unshakeable core and using them to reach your goals.

Purpose tends to come down to two things: the work that you do, and the passions you pursue.

The two don't always have to overlap, but more power to you if they do.

It's paradoxical on some level but this doesn't make it any less true: women are drawn to men who are willing to die for their purpose. Even though a woman knows that she will lose him, she will know that she lost him in pursuit of something greater than himself.

That in essence is purpose.

Although it is unlikely a woman would ever admit that she would let her man die in pursuit of what he wanted, she would be infinitely loyal and compelled to be with such a man.

Bringing this down to a more practical level now.

Think about your job and passions.

Have you ever met two people with the same job? One of them might speak positively about the job, what he's learning, and how he's contributing to the mission. The other person complains. Shoddy management. Annoying customers. Long hours. Meager paycheck. One is seemingly unstoppable, and when he talks about his job his eyes glow – they are present. They are alive and determined to crush it. The other person might as well be slaving in a coal mine somewhere.

Even if you don't have your dream job, you should always take pride in your work. Always. Whether you're scrubbing toilets or serving smoothies, you should always show up and do your best for whatever your station in life requires. Having negative feelings about your job can cloud your mind with negativity, and that will bleed over into how you feel about yourself and about the world.

So maybe you're not passionate about your job, and that's ok. But what if you don't have *any* passions?

Consider this: most people think passion comes before purpose, but it's actually the other way around. Passion often ensues from purpose.

Stop where you are, figure out where you can apply your energy, learn, and make a difference, then keep pursuing that activity. Studies have shown that as we develop skills and become good at things, we develop deep satisfaction from such activities.

Just because you're passionate about something doesn't mean you're skillful at it. Conversely, in many cases, developing competence or skill in something tends to foster the growth of passion and deep interest.

Think about it. When you've done something for long enough – when you hit that groove – it feels good.

The leading theory is something called Self-Determination Theory (SDT)[7] and it argues that anybody can love what they do so long as it satisfies these three criteria:

Autonomy: you have some control over how you spend your time.

Competence: refers to mastering things that are of use to you or someone else (i.e. a valuable service).

Relatedness: you have the feeling of connection with others.

---

[7] Deci, Edward L., and Richard M. Ryan. "The "what" and "why" of goal pursuits: Human needs and the self-determination of behavior." *Psychological inquiry* 11.4 (2000): 227-268.

So, if you focus on achieving these three things in your working life, a deep feeling of satisfaction or passion is sure to follow.

It may require a shift in mindset, but if you focus on learning, and getting better, you might find that you're more passionate than you thought.

Another way to explore what you're passionate about is to think back to when you were a kid.

What were the activities you pursued the most?

What kinds of things did you do for fun, with no regard for the end result?

Thinking back on the activities you did as a kid can help rekindle that creative spark and passion.

People who are passionate about things are radiant. They seem to exude positivity and enthusiasm, and people can feel this. People perceive passionate individuals as people who love life and are here to win and learn and savor every last minute of it.

It's so powerful.

I didn't know I wanted to be a coach, but when I found coaching it rocked my world. I love sharing useful knowledge and helping others grow. That's my purpose.

I've had people say "*Wow, there is something about you – you'll be successful*" when I talked about my passions (coaching, public speaking, videography, dating, travel, business) and often this was before I reached the level of success that I currently enjoy.

It doesn't matter where you are at currently.

I've been on the other side of the coin as well.

I've worked in terrible jobs I hated. I know for a fact that my vibe was completely different. I hated myself and ate junk food, drank a lot and let my issues get the best of me. When I felt like that, I certainly didn't attract anyone.

If you feel like that, you can't. It starts with having the belief that you can. You have to realize you can change it and it is realistic.

You can create a purposeful, rich life filled with women that cherish you and are spellbound by you. But it's up to you to make a decision to go for it.

No one else.

Purpose is more all-encompassing than just being about your career and passions.

Let me give you an example. Many of the men I have coached are decent men with integrity but have been ripped apart by bad relationships.

This is because they were slowly derailed from their purpose while in their relationship. You can think about this like an intravenous drip in the hospital.

One tiny drip of poison at a time will certainly ruin you over the long run.

This manifests itself as follows. The attributes that attracted their ex-girlfriends in the first place slowly fade away and become dormant. They cut off old friends and spend an increasing amount of time with their girlfriend.

They curb their ambitious, lofty goals for more 'realistic' ones.

They stop traveling, get a mortgage and decide that going to the gym is a waste of time. I.e. they become more submissive and give into the woman's needs more and more, until they no longer have the 'voice' they once had.

In short, they become complacent.

On a day-to-day basis these are changes that are quite small… small enough you won't even notice them. But over a decade, the compounded effect of these changes results in a complete transformation.

Again, while in the short term a woman may enjoy the man spending all his free time with her, eventually she will sense his lack of passion, zeal and direction. Things will stagnate, arguments will ensue, and eventually the relationship will be diminished because he didn't seek to challenge himself and do things that fulfilled him.

There are two options if you are a man that finds himself in that spot. You can blame the world and all its injustices or you can take responsibility and rekindle the fiery **purpose** you once had.

Being purposeful in your life will also prevent you from falling into another common trap. While many of you will not be approaching women, a small percent of guys and some dating 'gurus' adopt the 'mass approach' ideology. That is, approach as many women as possible and hope for the best.

They believe that dating is like a computer game, and hope that if they approach every living, breathing woman they might get a hit. Through sheer luck, this might work for some men, just because it gets them out of the house more than being an effective strategy.

For the vast majority of men this is terrible advice.

It is wrong for so many reasons.

For a start, if you have a purpose and vision in your life, the majority of your energy should be directed towards that. You should be pouring energy into what you love, not into approaching any woman you can in your spare time!

In the long term, the lifestyle of 'mass approaching' detracts from your core masculinity and attractiveness. As counter-intuitive as this sounds, bringing women into your life – particularly in a way that scatters your energy as much as mass approaching – diminishes your attractiveness.

You can trust me when I say this. This is coming from a guy who spent a lot of time approaching women!

Also, let's say you're a man that's fifty-five years old. Is it really appropriate and effective to go to the club, bars and street and mass approach as a successful strategy?

ATTRACTION DECODED | 69

No. We'll talk through the nuances of strategy later in the book.

On top of this, your success rate will be diminished and more and more time will be spent on approaching. The reason you yield lower results is because when you're mass approaching a couple things happen:

Firstly, your approach becomes disingenuous and fake. Women will sniff a rat. The quality women will sense that there is scripted nature and routine to this. It'll stop working as effectively and you'll dig deeper and deeper into the rabbit hole to find out why it's not working. You'll think it's technique or lack of knowledge or some nuanced point in self-development.

Please understand, I am not discouraging you from approaching. Please approach at will and every single day! But make sure you engage and approach women that you are *genuinely* attracted to.

If you do this, I promise something miraculous will happen. You will bring out your 'A' game.

Everything you say rolls off the tongue a little smoother, your jokes are a little bit funnier and you sincerely challenge her and bust on her. You have a great time in the process.

You both know it's real, not fake and she feels it deeply in her bones. She loves it and responds because of it. Sometimes she'll offer her number or take yours and will proactive chase you!

And if you don't get her number or she 'rejects' you, you can brush it off as it doesn't serve as a reflection of your intrinsic value or who you are; because you love your life!

The mass approaching guy gets butt hurt because he spends all his living hours approaching so it's going to make a difference to his perceived value in the world.

Too many people focus on cookie cutter techniques and mass approaching instead of focusing on one or two quality interactions throughout their day. The fact of the matter is, you get good at what you practice. Whether that is the first five seconds of the approach, or having deep, sexual, long and interesting conversations with women you really like.

If you get good at the latter, you'll be more at ease when it comes to women you are attracted to and cultivate the mindset of entitlement around beautiful women. You'll shift from thinking more about the technicalities of what to say and just be more at ease around beautiful women.

Again, there will always be some guys that twist what I say. This is not an excuse to sit and hide in the basement waiting for your 'perfect ten' before you get out and be social. You need to be approaching and engaging women. Period.

ACTION STEPS

List 3 things that you are passionate about in life. Pick one activity on your list you would sacrifice anything to pursue.

Ask yourself these questions:

- ❒ When you don't have much time, what do you always make time for?

- ❏ When you are talking, what topics energize you and fill you with enthusiasm or curiosity?
- ❏ When you don't have much money left, what do you always find money for?
- ❏ If money was not an issue, what would you do?

These kinds of questions help you identify your top values and passions in life. It's from those you will want to start a career or business around. Once you find that one thing, you need to set one big goal.

Once you have a big goal, you need to break it down into lots of little goals that you work on relentlessly until you accomplish all of them.

Right now, starting today for the next 30 days, use a pen and paper to write down a list of 3-10 goals for each day and execute on all of them.

The final thing I want you to do is write down how you feel when you wake up every morning. Do you feel happy and excited or sad? Motivated or uninspired? Aggressive/proactive or reactive/complacent?

Chapter Five

YOU WILL NOT WATCH PORN EVERY DAY

Porn does men no good.

It zaps you of your precious sexual energy, depletes you of motivation and leaves you feeling anxious and lazy.

Porn is like a drug and the more you use it the more addictive it gets. With the endless variety of scenes to choose from, it literally exhausts your brain from over-stimulation.

We did not evolve to see thousands of sex scenes at the click of a finger. The more you watch, the more you find yourself searching for something more to get your 'fix'.

Like bigger tits or that perfect round ass, and the less you find yourself motivated to talk to girls you see at the coffee shop or on the street.

I'm not advising you to settle for girls who don't 'look' like porn stars, I'm telling you your sexual attraction for women will literally drop as will your testosterone levels from overuse of porn.

The over-stimulation literally wreaks havoc on your hormones, causes anxiety, lowers your drive and removes the need for you to go out to meet real women. Guys who open their laptop every night to have a wank get laid less, it's that simple. Not only do men get laid less, you're fooling your innate genetic drive into believing you are reproducing. Your motivation to go out and approach women disintegrates the more you fool your body.

The worst thing about it all is that over the long term you're training your body to be 'satisfied' with porn and that it is normal and ok.

It can even cause erectile dysfunction in young men so when you do meet that cute girl at the bar you could have the awkward embarrassment of not being able to get it up if you somehow manage to take her home.

When you stop jerking off to porn you'll have a lot more energy to do the things you want to do.

In one of the best self-development books of all time, *Think and Grow Rich*, the author Napoleon Hill talks about sexual transmutation. This is taking that sexual energy and channeling it into purpose, drive, and your passions.

That immeasurable force that you use in sex can be transformed into a highly productive and potent form of energy for other things. I know that sounds a little out there, but try it.

By quitting pornography and masturbation your results and drive to get out there will explode.

Necessity is the mother of all invention.

You'll be inventing reasons to go out and socialize.

You'll want to go engage more women, you'll want to start that business or travel to new exotic places.

Motivation will go up in all areas of your life, as will your testosterone. Watching porn decreases testosterone while having sex with a girl increases it.

After you stop you'll never feel too ashamed to look girls in the eye.

You'll feel confident, more attracted to women and transfer that energy to them as you look them deeply in the eye with your primal instinct that radiates from you.

It's an easy decision.

For the next 30 days, while adopting these new habits and undertaking our 30-day challenge: you will quit porn and masturbation.

Quitting porn should be a permanent decision, not just a 30-day abstinence.

Instead, when you feel the desire to watch porn, channel that energy into a work project or get dressed and go out to meet real women.

A lot of guys swear by this idea of 'no fap'. Permanently quitting masturbating and refocusing that energy has become a huge movement. Google it.

Making this level of commitment to yourself is hard but I have seen tremendous results in people who have quit permanently. Even myself. In the long term, some of you might complain that quitting masturbation is too much of a drain and that science shows you have a healthier prostate and libido if you use it. I agree, that's why you should be having sex with real women.

If you do have to masturbate, do it once a week since your testosterone peaks on day 7. So instead of it being a 'time filler' when you're bored or a compulsive habit, pick a time and stick to just once a week. That's a much more powerful way of handling this.

ACTION STEPS

- ❒ If you watch a lot of porn, begin to taper down by watching more natural "artistic" videos, and not the sensationalized porn that is nothing like reality. Ultimately, you need to have completely quit over the next month and there is no other way around this. Stop watching porn.

- ❒ Experiment with masturbating from memories of your sexual history (think back to the visualization technique I taught you earlier). In a way, this will keep you more grounded in reality, so you won't need hyper-sexualized porn to turn you on.

- ❒ After the initial 'adjustment' period and removal from porn and masturbation, go all in with 'No Fap' and experience the true power of sexual transmutation and channeling your sex drive into going out meeting women in real life and working on yourself in other ways.

Chapter Six

YOU WILL STOP DRINKING ALCOHOL EVERY DAY

In my business, we call alcohol 'liquid state'.

Yes, it can instantly change your state, put you at ease and lower your inhibitions.

But do you really want to be that guy who relies on drinking to express himself?

That is not very alpha: it's the opposite.

You want to be naturally charismatic, fun and high energy without the booze.

What's more attractive to a hot girl in a nightclub? The drunk guy who is slurring his words and is completely uncouth, or the fun, sociable guy that is witty as hell and can pull the trigger and still leave her wanting more.

Uncouth behavior happens as a result of not understanding and reading social cues well enough. That can happen as a direct result of having drunk one too many martinis on any given night. The other interesting thing about being uncouth in your behavior is that it doesn't always happen because you're drunk (although this can be a big culprit). It can sometimes be because you're not picking up on clear social cues that are being put out. This demonstrates to others around you that you're not self-aware and therefore aren't in situations like this very often. You lower your value.

As a rule of thumb try to avoid uncouth interactions with people, unless it's intentional and for humor-based purposes, which is giving value.

Once you master going out without alcohol, you'll feel more confident and powerful. Knowing that you can go out and get laid any time you want without drinking is a powerful feeling. You can't rely on alcohol when you see her cross your path in the middle of the day or in the meeting when you need to give that presentation.

When you reach peak state without alcohol you usually have even more fun and it lasts longer.

To get there naturally, the secret is building social momentum. Talk to more people, have more interactions. To start with you will feel weird, but very quickly you will find yourself in a peak state.

There are three levels of confidence.
1. No confidence (A lot of guys will be sitting at this level).
2. Situational confidence (Some confidence in certain social situations or work situations).
3. Core confidence (Highest and rarest form of complete character confidence).

While having situational confidence is better than no confidence, it typically leaves you feeling really shoddy (i.e. only having the confidence to start a conversation with a woman at one particular bar, with one particular group of friends after at least a few drinks). Situational confidence is not the worst attribute to have but it does mean your ability to strike up conversations with women relies on a whole variety of external factors that are outside your control.

However, you take any person with situational confidence into a new environment and it's like watching a fish out of water. Flap. Flop. You see them flop and fail, and it's goddamn painful.

You should aspire to have core confidence.

Core confidence is being in any situation, at any time and having utter faith in your ability to do what needs to be done. It is the highest form of confidence someone can have.

What does it mean?

If you are sober at a bar, you can go up to the beautiful girl and her friends without hesitation.

If you are giving a presentation to 100 people, you can do it even though you may be nervous.

If you need to pitch your business idea to an investor, you can do it with relative ease.

Core confidence is a feeling of 'knowing' deep inside that you can trust in your character, even if the situation feels unfamiliar and you don't know a single person in sight. It means if you were dropped in any city or town in the world you could build a social circle, attract women and warm people with your presence. It means that you might not know how to do something but you have faith in your ability to learn. You can drop your ego and start as a beginner again in any activity, situation, or place.

That's real confidence and it's what you should aspire to have.

How do you cultivate such awe-inspiring core confidence?

It would take an entire book to write about the intricacies of cultivating such confidence, but with a few simple daily steps you will 10x your confidence in most situations.

You can start by making conversation with people every day, smiling more, asking the barista at Starbucks how her day is going. High five people. Have real conversations with strangers. When someone asks you "*How are you?*" you tell them straight up "*I'm awesome today, because…*" or "*My day sucks balls because…*"

This is congruence and people see your absolute ability to un-filter yourself as godlike. "There's a man with purpose who has no concern of what other people think". We respect people with congruence because even though their views may differ from ours, we admire people with the courage to share their unfiltered thoughts and ideas.

Even if they are nervous, emotional or just sharing something slightly controversial.

The more interactions you have with others the more your social muscle will build until eventually you'll forget why you ever drunk alcohol to begin with.

Giving up alcohol will also improve your sleep, raise your energy and make you feel better. Too much booze destroys your internal organs and it slows you down.

This chapter's cornerstone habit is withdrawing from alcohol for the next 30 days. I appreciate that you might want to have the occasional social drink. That's cool and not something I am necessarily against after the 30 days is up. However, the issue is when it becomes a crux to loosen up. Usually people loosen up using alcohol; if their life sucks, they have zero confidence and need it or they are depressed. You must decide on why it's so important to you.

ACTION STEPS

- ❒ If limiting alcohol is a challenge, start by setting limits for yourself: only x number of drinks on the weekend, and not at all during the week. Or, only 1 drink in social environments.

- ❒ Set a start date on your calendar and tell your friends about your 30-day challenge. That way there will be no surprises or temptation since everyone in your social circles will be in the know.

Chapter Seven

YOU WILL PROACTIVELY BUILD YOUR SOCIAL AND DATING LIFE

You picked up this book because your main goal is to improve your dating life.

So you'll be happy to know that I will share some of my best dating and attraction specific ideas in this chapter.

I also know that we've spoken about lots of topics that are correlated to your success with dating, but we have not discussed the specifics of dating techniques such as conversation starters, your vibe, and your energy when you meet women. These are crucial factors for you to work on and learn to improve your dating skills. Learning the ins and outs of dating while practicing what works for YOU is crucial. The reason I got better was because I went out there and tried. I tried different techniques and I experimented.

Sometimes I looked like a dummy who was clueless. I went home and cried and felt sorry for myself. But the next day I picked myself up and dusted myself off and tried again. And I kept trying until I started getting trivial successes and built off those successes. I built off those successes until I was getting good, consistent results and then those good results became incredible results. Those incredible results then became elite level results and after that I *still* kept going.

Compounding interest is a powerful thing. One little step today leads to massive change and growth in the future. Just focus on getting 1% better every single day.

Even if you feel stuck now, you can eventually get the results you want by taking consistent action in your dating life.

There's always more to learn and improve, no matter what level you're at: better body language, more effective ways to start conversations, deeper understanding of female psychology, more information on how to build your self-image and self-esteem. For some of you, it'll always feel like you need to know just a little bit more before you start acting. And while additional knowledge can sometimes be useful, you can't spend your life preparing for optimal situations – because they don't exist.

Reading and learning are great, but none of that matters if you don't take action and use that knowledge. There will never be a perfect time for you to start constructing your ideal dating and social life.

In this chapter, I'm going to highlight some of the most important ideas I've learned within dating itself and a few simple ideas to start to correct these 'issues' like looking at body language and some simple conversation starters to get you going.

You will notice several universal laws when you meet someone who is deemed an attractive man. After running hundreds of one-on-one consultations and meeting thousands of men at live seminars, I have seen no exceptions, so you ignore them at your peril. These laws are omnipresent.

> If you are willing to look at another person's behaviour toward you as a reflection of the state of their relationship with themselves rather than a statement about your value as a person, then you will, over a period of time cease to react at all.
>
> **YOGI BHAJAN**

I want to run you through a visualization.

Imagine you're walking down a busy street and you see a beautiful girl. Physically you find her super-sexy. Long flowing hair, glowing eyes and a smile to match. You're on the biggest and busiest shopping street in your city. There are people all around but you know deep down inside that you would love to go on a date with her. Right now you'd just love to have the courage to go up to her.

On a scale of 1-10 how scared of approaching are you? Write it down and be honest about it. Visualize it if necessary.

Now, imagine you're walking down that same street but all the shops are closed. It's early in the morning, the sun is out already. You feel the warmth on your face. The street is empty. Out of a side street this gorgeous girl catches the same stride as you. She's so close to you, you can even smell her scent. You're walking right next to her at the same pace. You can't believe it. Except for that one girl walking next to you there isn't a single soul around.

You feel the urge to approach again.

On a scale of 1-10 how scared of approaching are you now? Write it down.

Finally, imagine you're traveling. You're in some exotic place, think Africa or Asia. You're in the middle of nowhere. There is not even a town or a village, just a few people around. You decide to go on a hike for the day and you're looking forward to your day of nature and solitude. You're hiking in the middle of the grassland desert and out of nowhere this gorgeous girl walks over a hill and starts striding towards you. You're gobsmacked. She is now right in front of you and walking towards you.

On a scale of 1-10 how scared of talking to her are you?

Think about the last scenario in the grassland again, but this time when she walks past you she drops her wallet and you see her passport fall out. However she doesn't pick it up.

What do you do?

If you're a guy with any common sense, you pick it up and give it to her. But how anxious on a scale of 1-10 are you in that final scenario? Do you even think about anxiety or fear on a scale?

Write down your answers to each question before progressing. This is important.

Now, coming back to the last scenario. Did your anxiety register when you picked up a wallet and gave it to her?

No. Most guys I ask agree that they don't even consider it.

In those scenarios above, usually the anxiety goes from an 8 to a 5 to a 3 to a 0 or 1. What are the big differences in each of these scenarios? In each circumstance you're still engaging a beautiful girl and talking to her. The crazy thing is you can change the anxiety levels that you feel just by shifting the mental context of each scenario.

Let's dig a little deeper.

The first scenario, you're focused on taking. How do I approach her? What can I get from her? Can I get her number? How do I get in her pants? All those very familiar thoughts you probably experience on a daily basis when you see a beautiful woman. Those are taking, selfish or I-based thoughts. The fact you put so much pressure on yourself and are so inwardly focused creates anxiety and doubt. It also repels the people that you do finally have the courage to go up to. At this stage, you're effectively a value leach; looking for victims to mentally, physically and spiritually take from.

Let's look at the second scenario, in which we change just one variable – the amount of people around you. So if you experience a dip in anxiety from the first scenario to the second this is because you have a big fear of what other people think of you. You're worried about being embarrassed in front of other guys and girls. You may think that you're just scared of losing face with the girl. Most of my clients crave validation from male peers more than they want to appear cool and get the girl.

This is a horrible place to be. You're still seeking validation from other people on whether or not your actions are 'in'. You're looking at people to say it's ok for you to do what you want. You need their permission. You compare yourself to those around you. This may extend beyond dating and has terrible implications.

The third and fourth scenarios usually represent a huge shift in emotion and fear. The approaching of the woman in the rural grassland feels like a necessity.

To not speak to her would be weirder than to speak to her. The context of the situation has completely shifted. There are no judgmental eyes, no fear or anchored, negative emotions of being locked in your home city. Just you and her. Your curiosity here would be high. What is she doing here? Why is she here?

The final scenario represents the complete abolishment of fear. You simply pick up her dropped passport and hand it back to her.

You are still effectively starting the conversation, but this time in a genuine way with zero pressure. You're not selling yourself, or looking to take anything.

You've come complete circle. The only variables that have changed are the environment and context to which you've started a conversation with her. That's the big lesson I want to give you.

Changing the mental context from which you approach will drastically change your results and how you feel about striking up conversations with beautiful women.

What's the shift you are going to make?

Switching from being a *taker* to a *giver*.

Taking To Giving

You see, once you shift the focus off yourself and the other people judging your approach any perceived pressure starts to ease. Try to shift away from impressing her by solely selling yourself so that you can get her number, or have sex, or get her as your girlfriend. Shift your paradigm and you find yourself in the position of chooser.

Just take the *damn* focus off yourself for a change. The guys that give the most, in my experience, always have the most success with women. I am not talking about being a sugar daddy either. I mean the giving of emotions, experiences and ultimately value. People – both men and women – want to spend time with people who give emotional value.

Women are drawn in by the guys who do this. These guys aren't self-obsessed and riddled with insecurities. They are the guys at the bar that speak to and engage everyone. They can flirt with women they aren't necessarily attracted to, not just the beautiful ones. They can banter and have a laugh with the guys without feeling inferior or superior.

They can laugh at themselves, but enjoy teasing others too. They genuinely listen and are interested in others, not as some 'dating hack', but because they are interested and want to learn about the women they might date and the guys they might make friends with. They give without any expectation about it coming back, but it does come back, it comes back one hundred times over. They get invites to the best parties, people ask them to hang out, people love their company and they are often double and triple booked. They have boundaries, they don't simply give to those who take, take, take. They give value but they are not carpets for people to walk all over. In fact, the giving philosophy instills the opposite.

They are strong yet purposeful, but still give relentlessly. Giving is also a form of sharing your opinion, or challenging those around you. It's teasing a woman, challenging her and yourself to be sexually free and open. It's walking away from the women that have awful personalities and letting them know that just because she is physically attractive that is not enough for you. Maybe for someone with low standards but not for you. Giving is the highest form of social and dating ability.

"Well that sounds lovely for Disney World but what about the harsh practicalities of the real world. How exactly do I live that in a practical sense, Michael?"

It means when you see that girl on the street, you walk up to her and pay her a compliment. You give it to her, just to give. You have zero expectations of her wanting to continue the conversation afterwards. Your body should feel like it's walking away before she's answered. You're a busy guy with a lot of value to give in the world.

If she does stop and you vibe with her and appreciate her personality, you ask her out and you persist. You pull the trigger. If she is a bit nervous, you persist and put her at ease. If she turns her nose up at you, that's cool too because you would never have got on well with her anyway.

You don't place your intrinsic self-worth in the hands of some random chick just because she looks hot. Beauty is common. Have some standards for yourself. All attractive guys have high standards for themselves. If she isn't one hundred percent interested in hanging out, you can do something else. Build your business. Get that promotion. Go to the gym or even find someone more beautiful, with a better personality to hang out with you.

It takes ten seconds to pay someone a genuine compliment. Instead of being so damn selfish why don't you take the focus off yourself and do it?

It also means that you ask people that you come into contact with how their day is going. You listen and respond like a human not like a robot with automated responses. I don't care if it's the cashier at Starbucks, the barista, the receptionist, or the stranger on the bus. It means when you go out you introduce yourself to people you stand next to at the bar, just to make conversation. It means checking your ego at the door and learning that you're a human being.

It means when you approach women, you don't obsess about what you want. You're free of needing a specific outcome. Or even trying to 'control' how she feels towards you. Any outcome is fine as long as you express yourself honestly, true to your identity and values.

When you see a girl, you go over and have fun. You laugh at your own jokes. You laugh at her. She laughs at you. You give her great emotions whether that is being funny, positive, curious or just sexual because that is a form of giving too. I'm not asking you to pretend you're not interested in the girl, she craves to be desired. She wants you to tell her that she's sexy. Every woman thrives on that feeling of being desired by a guy she is attracted to.

Everyone wins.

This is not a mindset to adopt. Or a new piece of 'dating technology'. This is a way of life. In everything you do you should be bringing value to people's lives. The ironic thing is, the more you give, the more women that'll start to approach and engage you. The natural extension to our giving philosophy is the idea of *validating everyone*.

That means, making everyone you come into contact with feel positive emotions and validated as a human. After even a thirty-second conversation with you, they should feel like an awesome person that you're interested in. When I made this shift my results in business, with women, family, and friends literally tripled in the span of a month. It was ridiculous. Free coffees, meals, upgrades. More friends, dates, sex, invitations than ever before.

This is not a manipulation. This was just me deciding to truly share who I was and give.

Here is another powerful metaphor to help you internalize this concept.

Close your eyes and visualize yourself during the day in your city or town. You are the city's official lottery governor. When someone wins the lottery, you find them and surprise them with £10,000 or $10,000. Today you are giving the prize to a woman, who just happens to be gorgeous. You're in the city center and she's there at a coffee shop with her gorgeous friend. They're sitting there laughing, drinking lattes and generally having a good time.

How do you feel about going up and giving her the prize money?

Do you feel nervous?

Do you feel anxious?

Perhaps a little….

But, ask yourself honestly, would you feel like you were disturbing her?

For nearly 99.99% of people I've asked, they not only feel like they're not disturbing her but they WANT to go up and share this great news with her.

I mean who wouldn't want to win £10,000!

Just like the giving scenario above (in the desert with the passport), you are giving her something. You are giving the prize money to her.

Well, let me ask you this, how much do you value yourself?

If you had to, what monetary value do you put on youself?

Is it £5,000?

Is it £10,000?

£1,000,000? Or £1,000,000,000 even?

You're absolute worth cannot be measured, because you are priceless. What you bring to this world cannot be priced because it is truly unique and one of a kind.

So when you approach a woman, this is what you represent to her. A priceless gift. Although you won't be this to every woman you meet, to the right one(s) you could go on to become her future husband or long-term partner. You could go on to make her day, change her year, or even her life. This is why giving is not just optional but mandatory.

Shift away from being the 'empty cup' always needing to be filled up by other people's validation and start accepting that you have a great gift to give… yourself!

Switching from taking to giving is a monumental shift if you can internalize it. Even as you are reading this you can make a choice.

"Ah, whatever, I do this already, it's something I already know."

If that is how your internal dialogue sounds, maybe you're not ready for this yet.

"When the student is ready, the teacher appears."

Take some time off to digest what this means. Read those paragraphs on giving again and again and again till it clicks in your heart and head.

Or perhaps if you're lucky and open minded, you can literally feel your heart and gut churn with excitement as you understand the groundbreaking changes that will occur in your life over the next few weeks and how this will trickle into the very fabric of your life forever.

I promise you, if you start my 30-day challenge and take on board that philosophy your life will permanently change and you will never look back.

<u>Give value</u> every single day. Validate everyone.

Strategy

I'm about to blow your mind with something a little controversial.

Sure, part of the reason you're not successful with women might be because you're slacking in your physical appearance, or are afraid to approach. But one of the biggest reasons why your dating life sucks is because you lack strategy. Your dating life is something you've likely never intellectually tried to wrap your head around. You follow the standard pickup advice on where to meet women, how to approach them, and what to say.

Take peacocking for example. If you've ever read a single thing from a pickup artist, you know peacocking. For those who are unfamiliar, peacocking is a pickup technique where you wear one piece of rambunctious, loud, or flamboyant clothing. Maybe it's a ridiculous gold cane you carry with you. Maybe it's a zebra skin top hat. Maybe you wear massive, bright purple platform boots every time you go to the club. The idea is to draw attention to yourself with something so completely out of the ordinary that women can't help but notice you – like the plume of a peacock, so goes the rationale.

Now, what if you have terrible social anxiety? If you endeavor to avoid being in the spotlight in social situations, at all times? Well, then the peacocking strategy would work terribly for you, despite what Guru X tells you.

Peacocking does work for certain personality types, but certainly not others. And by extension, some guys do better with certain dating strategies, while others are best suited for something completely different.

All of the best seducers are usually EFFECTIVE in one method of attracting women. They pick the strategy that yields the greatest results and focus on that one area, getting better all the while.

I have one client who is analytical, methodical, and introverted. He works in IT and his job is pattern recognition. He struggles with approaching strangers and has a good amount of social anxiety, but that didn't stop him from *crushing* it online and he always has 4-5 dates lined up a week. Online dating worked for him because he's good at connecting through the written word. Peacocking would be an awful idea for this guy.

In stark contrast, I had another client who became a nightclub promoter. Although he had zero connections to begin with, he was outgoing, dressed trendily and loved hip-hop and dance. He went out and started small. Now, every night he is surrounded by gorgeous women. He's young, good looking and is very happy with his dating life. This fellow, to contrast our introverted IT friend from above, would probably adapt to the peacocking strategy pretty well.

Another example is a guy who is fun and outgoing. He loves to approach women in the street or coffee shops. He's the kind of person who makes friends everywhere he goes – a real social butterfly. And this strategy works with women too because they see him as a fun, sociable person, and he gets at least a number a day and several dates a week.

Honestly if I put the online-dating-crusher in a nightclub, he would be ridiculously outmatched and outgunned by the suave, smooth talking guys in there. The loud, bustling nightclub would make him clam up instead of coming out of his shell. The same thing would happen if I got the extroverted nightclub promoter to try online dating. He does great at approaching women because he has high verbal and social intelligence – he's great at speaking and connecting with people – and he's got some charisma. This same person would struggle in online dating. Why go through the trouble of learning to write a profile and decipher women's profiles if he's already capable of meeting women in his daily life?

Therefore, it is so important to understand who you are. You need to know where your strengths lie so you can pick the best strategy for you and focus on getting better in that one area. To start with, at least.

Anyone who is successful with women has a strategy, even if they don't consciously call it out.

In fact, in the scientific community these are called 'mating markets'. Instead of dividing your efforts across multiple mating markets, you just have to pick the one that suits you and your sensibilities the most.

The honest truth that dating coaches don't want you to know is that you don't need to be great at approaching women everywhere. In fact, if you were to try to be amazing at approaching women in every single environment you would be average in all of them. Average skills bring average results. If you're a guy that is struggling with women, then it would take you at least a couple of years to round off your skill level to the point where you would be able to get average results in *any* environment. If you're a man that is purposeful as we discussed earlier, why would you do that?

A lot of people that have seen my YouTube videos try to model my behaviors and attract women in every single environment. My strategy works well for me because I've been doing it for years, and it's a way for me to demonstrate certain techniques. It may work for you, it might not, but the bigger point is to focus on your unique strengths and identify the best mating market for you.

Which is the best mating market for you?
- ❒ Approaching women during the day?
- ❒ Approaching women in a bar or nightclub?
- ❒ Online dating?
- ❒ Cultivating and growing your social circle?
- ❒ Special hobbies and interests with sub-cultures, i.e. surfing?

Now, if you try and master attracting women in every single facet of the above mating markets, what will the end result be?

You'll be shoddy in all of them and will get lackluster results.

So what is my advice to you?

Pick the strategy that works best for you – pick your mating market.

Now, if you don't know which would work best for you, try them all. Experiment. Eventually, you will get a good idea of where you should focus your efforts to get the results you want. You need to cultivate self-awareness and understanding of what makes you unique, different and attractive. Understand yourself so deeply that you know which environment you have the potential to shine in. Think about the one method or place where you could CRUSH it.

If you're an athlete, think about developing your own method of meeting women at sporting events, perhaps after your game or at socials for the athletes.

If you're an introverted, quieter type of guy that doesn't like to go out so much but are smart and witty. Try utilizing online dating.

If you're social and naturally extroverted and love being around people, try building your social circle.

Each of these methods requires time to master, which is why it's best to focus on one.

Remember, playing to your strengths doesn't give you an excuse to be shy.

And you being strategic certainly doesn't equate to you staying in your room, swiping on Tinder all day either. It just means you are being real with yourself. Still find time to engage women in all places but try to become a master at one of the mating markets.

Round out your weaknesses and double down on your strengths.

Don't waste your time and energy trying to learn every nuance of conversation, escalation and approaching. You don't need to be the master of every single attraction skill in existence. A man that is trying to be purposeful in his life, to give his gift to the world doesn't have the capacity to. You can reach your dating goals quickly and effectively by understanding your 'mating market'.

Dump 99% of dating advice you read on the junk pile. Otherwise you'll get nowhere, fast. Focus on getting very good at one or two techniques and ideas instead of trying to become a jack of all trades. Focus on the core dating fundamentals that you need and move on. Pick your mating market, gauge progress, and revaluate as you move forward.

Body Language

Body language communicates a massive amount of information and it is one of the first things people will judge you on. It's science. Most people assume that they hold themselves effectively, but the fact is, unless you've deliberately examined your posture and body language, chances are you have much room for improvement.

A woman will look you up and down and size you up as a mating partner in 5 seconds. Ninety-five percent of her impression on who you are will be solidified within the first 30 seconds. After the first five minutes, her impression of you is pretty much set.

An attractive man needs confident body language. You can fake it, until your internal dialogue is congruent with your external image. But I've never seen a man with consistently good results with women display consistently poor body language. It just doesn't happen.

Understanding body language is important because it helps you read her signals too.

Women naturally have an edge over men when it comes to reading body language.

Everyone I ask assumes they are 'pretty good' at reading what someone else is thinking and feeling. The majority of men suck at this. There was a study done that shows that women are up to 3 times better at reading body language than men.

This is a huge difference.

A very smart guy named Albert Mehrabian did an experiment to see what percentage of people's thoughts and feelings come across from their body language, and this is what he found:

The way someone feels and thinks about you comes from this breakdown:

- ❐ 55% Facial expression and physical body language
- ❐ 38% Tonality and projection
- ❐ 7% Coming from the words you say

Think about that for a second. That means 93% comes from everything else besides the words you're saying. So we need to rethink what women really judge as attractive. Is it that fancy pickup-line you saw someone use in a YouTube video?

Wrong.

The most attractive people are sometimes quiet, sometimes loud and charismatic. They can be introverted or extroverted. But without exception. WITHOUT exception. I have never met a man that is attractive without him having strong and effective body language.

Here are five ways to improve your body language starting today:

Eye contact

Maintain eye contact: most guys are weak sauce at this. Failing to maintain eye contact indicates insecurity, or an inability to open-up for connection. Women want that guy that will look them square in the eye and make them feel butterflies in their stomach. They want to meet the guy that finally is unafraid of their beauty and whose eye contact pierces to her very soul. Maintaining steady eye contact shows you are present, confident, and eager to connect on a deep level.

A lot of guys get put in the friend zone. It's one of the most commonly brought up problems when I run 1 on 1 coaching and consultations. How do you communicate sexual desire with just your eyes?

Well, there are many more subtleties of eye contact that people don't understand. There is a lot of underdeveloped science around eye contact that I am sure will come out in the near future. She can feel what you're thinking and where your mind is at when you're looking at her dead in her eye. Stop being apologetic about wanting her and show her your desire through your eye contact. The number one thing she wants to feel is desired. If you can't look at her like you want to have sex with her. Do you think she'll feel like a woman?

Tension

There is a natural tension that exists between a man and women when there is mutual attraction.

When you are on a date and you look a woman deep in her pretty eyes you feel it. It's this thick, dense feeling that fills the bubble you're both in. Your job is simply to live in this bubble by being present and engaged.

One of the critical aspects of building attraction is to focus on the woman. Don't be distracted by other people at the bar or restaurant. Just like meditating is about focusing on breathing, doing well on a date is about engaging the woman, being present with her in that bubble, and making her feel like she has your full attention. In these moments where both your eyes are locked, your job as the man is to let that tension brew. When there is a silence, don't 'snap' the tension despite how awkward you may feel. Those tension building moments are golden opportunities to project your lust and desire onto her. She'll feel this deep inside. It'll make her feel womanly and sexy. Don't break into conversation, laugh or grin nervously. Sit with it; that deep eye contact, and let it simmer. If the tension is too much for her, let her break the tension and calibrate your behavior to match hers. If she doesn't break eye contact in this moment, she usually wants to be kissed or more.

Maintaining eye contact is an important way to escalate sexual tension, but so is how you direct the conversation. Sometimes saying less is actually saying more.

This is how you should approach it:

Whenever you're on a date, you should never be exclusively focused on the goal of having sex with her or making out with her, even if that's what you want. That puts too much pressure on you, and will make you do something stupid, say something dumb, or fail to exist in the moment and genuinely connect – ultimately sabotaging the thing you probably want the most.

Instead, your goal should be to have fun, ask questions and where appropriate let the tension simmer as we mentioned above.

If you don't know what to talk about, pretend like the woman has a secret talent that nobody knows about. Your mission on the date is to ask her questions about herself and "dig" to find out what that is. This shows how interested you are, how engaged in the conversation you are, AND, even though she will be doing most of the talking, she'll think you're an amazing conversationalist and listener.

This builds incredible attraction, trust, familiarity, desire, and other positive emotions.

So many gurus will recommend you try conversation hack 'X' or 'Y' to increase your chances with women. My recommendation is start with honesty, authenticity and presence.

i.e. There is no need to brag about your 'higher value'!

A man that is attractive has implicit value and as a woman gets to know him this seeps out naturally over time. She will sense how different you are to other guys around her vying for her attention.

Your humbleness couples with the value that organically unfolds as a result of her getting to know you will make her want to chase you.

Women are hyper-aware of gimmicks and gambits you try to use; they've effectively spent their entire life learning how to deflect men's advances.

Posture

A lot of you will work or study at desks. Or have improper posture for some of the day. Some of you literally look like the hunchback of Notre Dame after a few hours in the office every day.

Get to work on your posture with squats, deadlifts and compound lifts. None of this slouching over stuff. It screams of poor social awareness and 'leave me alone' I need to ring a bell in a clock tower in a dark church somewhere.

Posture is so important but it is synonymous with your presence. When you're with a woman she wants to feel like she is in the presence of a man. A purposeful man who charges in on his day. Not a slouch. If you can't even own the way you walk and stand, what signals do you think you send her about the rest of your life?

Also, have a think about if your body is closed off (i.e. not approachable) or open. This will drastically shift how many people engage you socially. If a pretty girl sees your amazing presence across the bar, looks you up and down and takes a fancy to you, she'll look and try to catch your eye as she goes by.

If your back is turned towards her or you have a scowl on your face it will make her feel less likely to come over and engage with you. Instead of that, imagine you have a twinkle in your eye and a cheeky smirk that screams: "Come over, it'll be fun". Hell, who knows? She may even come over and chat with you.

Tip:

Stand up, head held high. Now clench your fists as if you were holding a pencil in each hand. Pull your shoulders down and back, and chest up until the pencils are parallel and pointing straight in front of you. If you have poor posture, the pencils will naturally want to face inward, towards each other. Use this cue for better posture throughout the day until it becomes habit. Chest up. Head held tall. Shoulders down and back.

SMILE

First thing's first: you need to be able to smile.

Do you know what smiling actually signals to a woman? Kindness. Openness. Empathy. Happiness!

Now consider what a scowl or frown signals. Standoffishness. Closed-off. Possibly anger. Maybe irritable. Certainly not happiness.

Smiling at women simply puts them at ease. It signals that you're a friend not a foe. Women want to be around men who are happy, and open, and kind – all of which a nice smile can signal.

Smiling is certainly one of the master keys of facial expression. But nothing trumps the importance of **range**.

The most attractive guys aren't the men who are dead-pan or the ones that are smiling all the time. The most attractive men have what I call the full range of expression.

You can smile. You can laugh. You can look mean. You can look at her seductively with a straight face.

It's not about one method or 'way' of coming across. It's about having the ability to express the full range of emotions and being self-aware in how you're expressing your face at any moment. If you're a guy that looks bored all the time even though you're engaged, this is a blind spot you need to fix. If you look serious or even angry all the time, again this is something you need to address. If you laugh or smile nervously, again this is an involuntary behavior which is not in alignment with your thoughts and feelings and this is where a lot of the issues with men's facial expressions come from. Supplicating facial expressions turn women off and are a very real problem I see on a daily basis.

VOCAL USE

Do you mumble your words or do you project them loud and clear? Do you alter your pitch, or speak in monotone? If you approach a woman but are whispering she will assume you are scared of sharing your thoughts with her and the world. It's not just about your projection but also the tonality with which you say things. If you say things with a downward-sloping pitch at the end, that is an assertive, confident tone.

"*You look beautiful*" sounds very different in a downward-sloping assertive tone than if said in an ascending tone like you would ask a question "*You look beautiful?*" Imagine being a woman in a coffee shop reading your copy of Fifty Shades of Grey, waiting for your own charming, confident Mr. Grey to approach you and just as you look up, standing before you is a guy who looks the part. Well groomed, strong presence, but when he talks, his voice says he is constantly looking for approval.

Even in his first words. "*You look beautiful?*" she realizes. He may be nice. He may even be funny. But he'll never be able to make me feel sexy and desired. He's too unsure of himself.

Now imagine the guy that strides across the room and tells her she is sexy and he wants her. It may be a bit over the top and forward; he may even be an absolute asshole. But she responds. That dominating tonality sets her loins on fire. The variance of your tonality is important too. It's not just about being loud and dominating. If you say everything like that, you will end up sounding like Arnold Schwarzenegger in The Terminator. It's all about varying your tonality: use pauses and silences as tools to build suspense; use the minimum number of words to get your point across.

So the keys here are to project, using the full capacity of your mouth, lungs and diaphragm. Enunciate your words but don't overdo it and seem fake. Your authenticity takes a hit if you do this. Be mindful of your tonality. Limit the use of the seeking-approval tonality. Default to the dominant tonality to get across your compliments, ideas and statements. Don't forget to use pitch variance and avoid monotonous sounding voices.

As a side note, the best conversationalists are never the ones that talk the most, they're the best listeners. I don't care how amazing of a storyteller you are. It will never beat the person that listens effectively. When we feel someone is intently hanging off every word and giving us their undivided attention, we cherish that. Being a great listener is the key to having a great connection with someone. Responding to their words reassures them you are truly engaged with what they're saying. It's a magical experience for both people in the conversation.

PHYSICALITY

It is a lot harder to form an intimate connection with a woman without reaching over and establishing physical contact. Scientific studies have shown you're twice as likely to get compliance from someone you touch. So you're twice as likely to get a girl's number if you reach out and touch her.

The simplest touches to incorporate are:

- ☐ Hugs, handshakes.
- ☐ Placing your hand on her shoulder as you talk to her.
- ☐ Perhaps a little nudge as you tease her as you walk down the street.
- ☐ Being curious about tattoos, clothing, earrings, nails or anything on her body gives you an excuse to reach out and touch.

I appreciate the first touch can be awkward as hell. But the longer you leave it, the worst it gets. If you're super-awkward and unlucky you might achieve the slam dunk of awkward touches: lunging out for a kiss at the end of the date and her having this 'omg, he almost touched my lips' look on her face as she pulls back. Don't worry, even I have experienced this. While it was painful in the moment, it taught me that I could avoid that awkwardness on future dates by gradually building up my touching and physicality.

Physical touch is like a dance and it requires some situational awareness. At first you start with fleeting touches. Then as your connection increases you begin to touch her for longer periods, and for more consistent lengths of time that will eventually turn into you holding her. Having your arm around her. Stroking her face, the small of her back. Grabbing her hands. Be playful with it. If she pulls back after your initial touches, use common sense, but don't give up.

Sometimes when a woman isn't ready to be touched, it doesn't mean no. It just means that she is not ready yet and you need to focus more on the connection between both of you[8]. My slightly controversial rule is to physically increase your touching as quickly as possible and wait for her to pull back a little bit. This is because most guys I coach are like turtles in their shell. The woman is waiting and waiting. She is attracted to them. She wants them, but she waits and waits and waits. By the time he is finally, one hundred percent sure she is ready to be kissed or to have sex, he has lost his chance. Her mentality being: "I have tried to show him how obviously head over heels I am for him, how much I want him, but he is just unbelievably oblivious. I give up."

Of course there are many more nuances of body language. If you want to be an attractive guy with a healthy dating life, you need to have body language nailed.

If you want to be an attractive guy with a healthy dating life, you need to have body language nailed.

You need to invest time in challenging your fears with women by speaking to them. There is no way around this. Even if your mating market is online dating, you're still going to have to learn how to speak with women on dates.

It all comes down to you and a woman exploring a connection. That is the pinnacle you're building up to.

If a man is living by all these lifestyle and behavioral habits but is not engaging women is he truly attractive?

---

8   Except for sex – if she says no, back off. She may playfully give you a bit of resistance when you touch her at a bar or on a date but rape isn't a joke. So when I say back off, I mean it.

Directly or indirectly, you need to build experience and comfort engaging with beautiful women. It will also strip you of any inflated ego issues. (Getting rejected by beautiful women tends to have that effect.)

Stripping your ego down also means that you don't allow your fear to come in through the back door and tell you 'I'm too good for X woman'. I'm too busy to speak to that woman over there by the bus stop because I'm 'on my purpose'. This is your ego coming in through the back door. Approaching women gives you a reality check and it makes you understand that no matter who you are or what your background is or how much 'self-development' work you've done you are still a beginner and you are still learning. You may get successes, but this will strip back any inflated feeling of importance and make you realize that, yes, you can meet women any way you want. Yes, you can be the attractive guy you want, but you've got to put in work and go up to them.

You need to fumble, mess up, get sweaty palms. Get anxiety. That's how you know you're truly in the game.

Try new things in different situations. Remember, I'm not asking you to become a master of all these individual dating situations; that is unnecessary to reach your dating goals. What I'm asking you to do is look for opportunities where there is a low-risk, high-reward.

Talk to women in your social groups, where it is easy, convenient, and a natural thing to do. Try online dating – you don't even have to leave your room immediately if you have too much social anxiety. Low risk with the potential for a high reward.

However, if you expect women to come up to you and start conversations, you're literally asking her to change her genetic wiring to be the one taking the lead. Instead focus on what is in your control: your mindset and attitude towards initiating conversations.

Occasionally a woman may start a conversation with you, just as you may win the lottery one day. But you wouldn't rely on the latter to guarantee financial freedom so why rely on the former to get the dating life you want?

In other words, don't assume you'll hit the jackpot, but humor the idea and be open to the opportunity, should it present itself.

Think of it as an unexpected prize. If it presents itself, savor it. If not, always remember you'll be fine without it.

Another common question I get is: Where is the best place to meet the best women? I'm hoping you figured that one out on your own after we dissected your dating strategy.

A better question to ask yourself is, what are you looking for in a woman that you want to date and where would *she* hang out?

There are amazing women everywhere and, chances are, the right woman for you will frequent the same places you already go. They'll like doing things you like to do.

A good exercise is to write down the qualities of the woman or women you want to meet.

Whether you're looking for short-term, medium-term, or long-term dating, you can have your pick as long as you go to where these women are. If you are just looking for short, casual encounters that is fine. Don't let anyone tell you it's not. And likewise if you're looking to settle into a relationship.

The point I'm trying to make is, if you're looking to meet a healthy, enlightened, non-drinking, non-smoking fitness model, you're unlikely to find her at the dive bar at the corner of your street.

Here's a chart on how couples most often meet their partners:

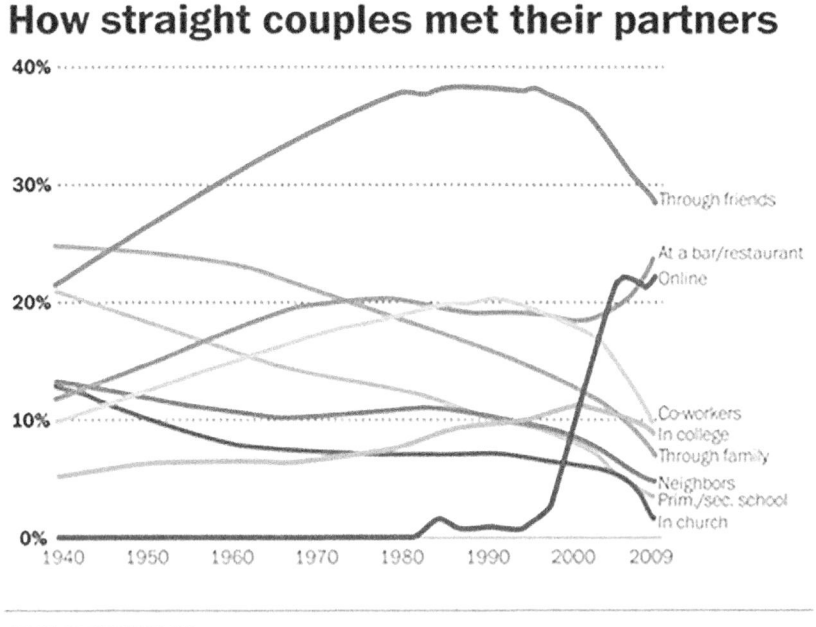

How straight couples met their partners

WAPO.ST/**WONKBLOG**
Source: Searching for a Mate: The Rise of the Internet as a Social Intermediary

The most common way people meet their long-term partners is through friends, at just under thirty percent. Randomly meeting

114 | MICHAEL VALMONT

women at a bar or restaurant or 'anywhere' is next at just under 25%, with online dating on the rise at 22-23%.[9]

Although this data is a little dated [2015], the point still remains: you *can* meet a woman anywhere you want to. This is why it's so important to equip yourself with the skills to meet women, but more importantly to pick the best strategy that would complement those skills.

If you don't want to be in late-night venues such as bars and clubs, approach women during the day; in the coffee shop, at the grocery store, in the museum. Think about where the girl with your value system would spend her time. You'll usually find it will be in a place similar to where you like hanging out. A lot of guys initially are hesitant to approach during the day because they think women are busy, or it's creepy, or you're disturbing them. These are all just insecurities you are projecting on to them.

If a woman is single, there isn't a day she wakes up and doesn't want to be swept off her feet.

That's why she dolls herself up to go to the supermarket to pick up bread, and why when she goes to the gym she still has a full face of make-up. A big part of femininity is the search for a loving partner or sexual partners.

The great thing about approaching during the day is, it's different. In a bar or club the women are usually expecting it. You approach

---

9   Rosenfeld, Michael J., Reuben J. Thomas, and Maja Falcon. 2015. How Couples Meet and Stay Together, Waves 1, 2, and 3: Public version 3.04, plus wave 4 supplement version 1.02 and wave 5 supplement version 1.0 [Computer files]. Stanford, CA: Stanford University Libraries.

her during the day, it's something unique and special and you will immediately grab her attention. Even the most gorgeous girls, models, and celebrities will respond because they will feel like you are a man with balls who has put himself on the line.

Even if she has a boyfriend or is busy, it'll take you 15 seconds to start the conversation. It's a complete win-win situation. Even if she brushes you off. You become better in the process. You cultivate a thicker skin, you improve your social skills, you reward yourself for taking action. Even in rejection you get better and feel better.

I onced walked up a stunning actress. One that is well known and has done some popular TV shows. Even though she is at the top of the pecking order when it comes to social skills and circle, she melted because my daytime approach is so different to what she is used to.

I'm not saying that to brag. These are results you can experience for yourself too.

Some guys view approaching women during the day, as 'day game'. If it becomes a routine, then you lose the magic and the feel of it all. Women will sense this. Try to make it spontaneous, real and non-scripted. You're not a cookie-cutter man so don't make her feel like you're using cookie-cutter lines.

Just by walking up to her, you are already beating 9 out of 10 guys. You're in the top ten percent just by virtue of having the balls to approach her.

If you're a social butterfly, then cultivate a social circle of friends through connections. You'll get invites to tons of social invites, events, interesting parties and gigs. You'll meet loads of people and probably throw some cool parties yourself. People will want to spend time with you and you'll end up attracting the kind of woman that you want to meet.

If you're young and love music and the nightclub scene, think about being a promoter or at least forming associations with them. Approach women and bring them out to clubs with you. Demonstrate your social value when you're out and about having a good fun time and you will attract women.

I know it may feel like there is a big obstacle to do any of these things – approaching a woman during the day or getting started at online dating, for example – especially to the voice in your head. But as a pretty successful guy I know used to say…

If you hear a voice within you say "you cannot paint", then by all means paint and that voice will be silenced.

VINCENT VAN GOGH

If you want to go ahead and become the most attractive version of yourself you need to be engaging attractive women and you need to do it regularly. Every single day if possible. No excuses. You need to cultivate skills such as starting up conversations and doing so with honesty. It'll be great for you to cultivate female friendships too, but I know the reason you picked up this book was so that you could have more than that. When you meet new women, you need to get across the message that you are a sexual being and then learn the process of taking her home and then getting into relationships. That is a truly attractive man.

Remember, we're not talking about mass approaching. We're talking a few quality interactions on a regular basis. Think quality over quantity. Your engagements with beautiful women according to your dating strategy could be part of your social circle or club. It could be on dates that you've arranged via online dating or even at the bar. You just need to get comfortable around women you find very attractive.

This is something you'll have to play by ear, but in essence, you should absolve yourself of any "spray and pray", numbers game thoughts you have, and adopt a more selective lens in which you view potential romantic interests in your dating life.

We all have insecurities and limiting beliefs about ourselves. We think we're too short, or too tall. We think our skin color, or the way we look makes her unattracted to us. We think our accent is too thick or our voice isn't deep enough. We want to have a different eye color, or face, or hair color. I've seen a lot of my clients struggle with this, as have I. I want you to understand something.

You are enough as you are.

You may not feel it or believe me. That's fine. But just entertain the idea that you are. If you can accept your faults and insecurities, something crazy happens. All the things that make you feel insecure; you start to own them.

Your insecurities turn from a source of weakness into something which makes you stand out, in a good way. It makes you different and women love that. They tell you it's cool or funny simply because you own it. I used to have women tell me I was gangly and lanky, then I started owning it and now every woman I meet tells me she loves my height. Just because I started owning it as part of my identity and believed that I am enough as I am. All the things that make you feel insecure; you can literally turn them from a source of weakness to unique selling points.

Countless men I've worked with have huge handicaps. Diseases, missing limbs, in a wheelchair, blind, deaf. Guess what? They enjoy incredible love lives just because they didn't give themselves a good enough excuse. What about you?

Also, realize that as a woman, she has much more pressure on her to look good and will likely be much more insecure about her body shape, her face, etc.

Being an introvert isn't a good enough excuse either. Sorry. So many people make the mistake of thinking that being an extrovert means you are not shy and that being introverted means you are shy. I've had so many guys say to me that this is 'just the way they are'. It's just an excuse. Shyness is a socially learned habit. It's not an excuse to hide away in your basement with no friends and no dating life. The loudest, most outgoing guy at the party or bar can be an introvert. It's just how they use their energy to recharge that is different. You don't even need to be massively non-shy to get the girl you want either. That's not a necessity. But you do need to have the courage to get out there and start meeting women.

There is an endless amount of work you can do on yourself as we've mentioned above. A lot of this will take several years to conquer but understand this, you are enough as you are to meet that dream girl right now. You're on your path to becoming your best self and that's what she wants to recognize. She doesn't want the complete product, she wants ambition.

So from today onwards you are making a declaration that says you will approach and speak to at least 3 new women every day. It doesn't matter if that is at night or during the day. You will do it. That's over 1,000 new conversations with attractive women every year. Just think about the compounded effect that'll have on your skill set over the next several years.

ACTION STEPS

- ☐ Take an A4 piece of paper and create two columns, one with all your strengths and one with all your weaknesses. Ask friends and family for direct and honest feedback if necessary to help fill in any blind spots you may have on yourself.
- ☐ Write down the personality traits you're looking for in an attractive woman, identity the place where you may be able to meet her.

- ❐ Armed with your strengths, weaknesses and the kind of woman you desire. Figure out where you will focus your attention and efforts to get dates with women you desire. Build your dating strategy and spend 1-2 hours outlining exactly how you will be more effective in dating as a result. Understand you might not choose the right method at first but keep going with it

- ❐ The key methods that my clients have found most effective are:
  - Random Daytime Encounters
  - Developing their Social Circle
  - Going to Bars & Clubs
  - Online Dating
  - Through Clubs and Hobbies

- ❐ Interact with 3 different women every day. It can start as simple as a "hello", or a full conversation. The point is to get comfortable interacting with women wherever you go until it becomes second-nature.

- ❐ Practice holding direct eye contact with people. Make a game out of it and make eye contact with people on the street, cashiers at the store, or anyone else you come into contact with. You'll notice most people have trouble maintaining eye contact. Make them break contact first.

- ❐ Every morning before leaving the house make sure you have good posture. Practice smiling and making a range of facial expressions (think of it as warming up), and try reading aloud a few pages from a favorite book to practice good speech habits.

Final Chapter

CONCLUSION AND CHALLENGE

The next couple sections of the book are vital. They explain how I put all the strategies together so you get the results you want from your life and I suggest some additional resources that could be hugely beneficial. Make sure you read right to the end as on the last page we have a full list of internal and external changes we want you to make. This serves as a handy reference.

Also, just remember that the real results come as a result of implementing the information, not just acquiring knowledge. You're not a library. Your results are waiting on the other side of the 30-day challenge we've outlined for you. See the next steps in this chapter.

One of the most important lessons of this book and one that is omnipresent in all great self-development advice:

You must be persistent.

Unfortunately, if changing your life was easy, my job would be redundant and no one would need advice. It would be as simple as breathing and we would live in a perfect world where no one had flaws.

To give you some added motivation I thought I would share a story with you.

I was in my early twenties and things were going very well for me. I had just got a job out of university and was working diligently on my dating and social life, with great success. I was in a relationship with a beautiful Swedish girl whom I thought was 'the one'. We'd been together for a year and a half and I decided to go traveling for a while. I was on top of the world. I had new-found confidence. It seemed all this self-development advice had paid off.

While I was traveling, one night I got drunk and ended up sleeping with someone else. I immediately regretted it and told her instantly.

Shortly after this I fell ill with a severe allergic reaction and ended up in hospital in a third-world country. I burned through all my savings and came out of hospital one week later, alive, but still very physically sick. During my stay in hospital my girlfriend had decided that I wasn't worth the trouble and she ended it with me. I was in emotional and physical agony. I had that horrible, gut-wrenching pain of heartbreak. It hurt like hell.

I was flat out broke, but decided that I should try to win her back. I'd fly back to London in a romantic gesture and show her how much I cared about her.

So I borrowed $800 from my friend to fly back early. Crippled with anxiety, I surprised her outside her workplace. And she was shocked but not in a good way. She had already started seeing someone else. I crumpled to the floor and left embarrassed with my tail between my legs.

I went home and took stock of my life.

I was jobless, physically and mentally unwell, and penniless. My bed was now my mum's couch. To add to all of that my emotions had taken a battering. I felt sorry for myself and wrote in my journal for thirty days straight about what a pathetic loser I was. I tried to get out of this horrible depression but I couldn't. I didn't know where to start. But I started with tiny steps and despite the ups and downs I kept moving forward.

I wrote goals and I pursued everything that I wanted in my life. I began to ask myself the question: Why not me? If I'm going to feel sorry for myself and be a victim and say "Why me?" for the bad stuff I have to say "Why not me?" when it comes to the good stuff too.

Why not you?

The reason I'm telling you this is because I want you to understand there will be highs and lows in your journey. But the lowest lows do not compare to the highs I've had since then. Without that experience, I would not be the person I am today. Looking back, those experiences were some of the best that could have happened. I needed that kick up the backside to go out and grab life by the horns.

You're going to go through cycles of expansion and contraction. Sometimes you'll be meditating, visualizing, crushing your dating life goals, expanding your business empire and you'll suddenly take a misstep. Then that misstep will become a miss week, then month, and before you know it; you'll be in a slump. But understand this. The up will return and the down will fade. Always aim for consistency and persistence above all else. Always apply your smarts and strategy to your journey and that will take you a very long way. Be persistent. Endure. Come back to the morning ritual. Come back to prioritizing your appearance and well-being. These are the tools that will help you bounce back from a slump.

If you fail on your first date, try again. If you fail in your first presentation, don't give up at the first hurdle. Keep going.

If you approach the 30-day challenge with the mantra of massive action. You'll get insane results. If you approach it with skepticism and resistance you won't get the results you want.

I've created a complete list of shifts you need to make at the end of the book. I've also made a poster for you. Make sure you utilize this and do every single exercise I've suggested in the book. By using the physical check boxes on the poster, it helps you build habit momentum. There is a science here, the reward centers of the brain begin to release increasing amounts of dopamine as you start racking up the ticks. It's also good to see it every day to remind you of the mission you're on. You should treat this with urgency. Don't wait to start it. Remember there is no perfect time to start doing this.

Start today.

You're also probably thinking, that is SO much to implement over the next thirty days. Well, that's why I've constructed this 30-day challenge in a very special way. Habits such as not drinking or not watching porn – those are habits that require zero-time investment. They require discipline, but they will not actively require more of your day. Some of the habits will require you to prioritize your day a bit differently, but if you are looking for results in your dating life ultimately you have to decide precisely where your priorities lie now. Work and other priorities have likely landed you in the situation you are in.

I hope the initial results of this 30-day challenge encourage you to realize your full potential and you become the best version of yourself in every single way. I hope you create adventure and bring audacity back into your life. I hope you have successes with dates, socially, and in work, but most importantly I hope you screw up. Seriously. I hope you fail spectacularly. After you've failed, I want you to get back up and keep going. Complete the challenge despite adversity, because it's that resistance that builds the attraction skill set. It's with that adversity you can overcome the resistance to become your most attractive self.

Finally, I hope you take that leap of faith, complete the challenge and then decide to make this a lifetime challenge. A lifetime of dedication to enrich your life, build incredible relationships with women and build a bold and empowering social circle because ultimately:

Happiness is best when shared.

NEXT STEPS

I hate when you read a book that is filled with incredible life changing knowledge but there is no follow-up plan on how to apply what you've learnt.

It's for that reason, I designed the *30-day challenge poster* to accompany this book. The poster is designed so that you know what you need to do every single day to build the habits I've spoken about. If you truly commit to the daily activities I've outlined, I believe in 30 days you will feel significantly different. Your confidence will change drastically, your self-esteem will go up, and you'll have a thriving dating life or at least be making progress.

My personal recommendation is to run through the challenge at least 3 times consecutively with 1 week breaks in between. This way you get a 'rest' week in between. I've also set you some one-off activities to help you progress over the next 6 months. These are activities you can do to aid your growth, long term. These activities take around one to five hours to finish.

The poster focuses on long-term change; the opposite of the 'magic pill' quick fix that is perpetuated by today's society. I focus on improving one percent every day.

I've designed a beautiful A2 poster to put on your wall. Seeing that on your wall every day will reinforce your long-term goals and vision. The poster is only (UK)£15 + shipping .I ship this poster worldwide, so do not worry if you are based in America, Australia, Asia or anywhere else in the world!

Grab it here:

http://michaelvalmont.com/30-day-challenge-poster

I STRONGLY recommend you get the poster. Trying to implement the advice in the book is difficult without structure. So please go and grab the poster if you are committed to becoming your most attractive self.

If you can't afford the fifteen pounds for the poster, I offer it for free as a PDF - here. This is not as effective as the physical poster but still very useful.

GET IN CONTACT

Congratulations, on completing the book and taking action. I believe it is my mission to help men and women around the globe to achieve their potential in dating and in life.

So, it would really help if you were to review this book on Amazon. Your encouragement may help get my next book released more swiftly!

Please do that now, it'll only take a few minutes of your time.

I would also love to hear from you. You can send me your goals and vision for yourself. I may not be able to personally respond to every email but I assure you I will read them all:

mike@michaelvalmont.com

If you wanted to accelerate your learning and growth more rapidly and need personalized attention and feedback, I offer various courses and 1 on 1 coaching for those who want to make their confidence, dating and success a priority. We have intensive 7-day programs for international clients and 6-week programs for clients in the UK. These are programs that we have refined year after year with hundreds of clients. The process is truly transformational, so if you are serious about attracting women, get in touch.

You can request a completely free 1 on 1 consultation with myself or the team at my website: michaelvalmont.com

If you prefer you can also call us directly and someone from my team will get back in contact with you.

+44 20 8144 3121

This UK line is open 24/7, so if you're calling internationally don't worry, your call is welcome anytime.

Furthermore, if you want access to more free information, ideas and blog articles, don't forget to check out:

https://www.michaelvalmont.com

ABOUT THE AUTHOR

Best known for his strategic, no-nonsense, results-driven approach, Michael Valmont is one of the world's leading dating coaches. Michael's mission is to share only the very best information with men all over the world to create lasting results with women, with business, and with life. He has worked with multimillion-dollar companies, entrepreneurs, veterans, doctors, celebrities, and everyone in between. Simply put, Michael transforms lives.

Michael has been featured by over a dozen media outlets worldwide including BBC, The Guardian, Glamour, Men's Health, The Independent, and Sky News.

He has been a featured writer for some of the biggest online dating websites including Match.com, eHarmony.com and POF.com . He leads sold-out seminars with hundreds of clients and motivated men from all over the world, and has a popular YouTube channel that has garnered over 8 million views.

Average Man to Attractive Man shifts

AVERAGE MAN	ATTRACTIVE MAN
Negative outlook	Positive outlook
Hits snooze button every morning	Jumps out of bed with passion
Unhappy	Happy
Expresses complaints	Expresses gratitude
Lacks purpose and goals	Lives purpose and goals
Complacent	Ambitious
Reactive	Proactive
Passively absorbs information	Curates information that makes him better
Avoids fear	Faces fear
Out of shape, sedentary	In shape, active
Poor diet	Healthy, nutrient-rich diet
Dresses poorly	Dresses well
Poor, careless grooming habits	Good, attentive grooming habits
Jerks off instead of meeting women	Meets women instead of jerking off
Uses alcohol to dull anxieties	Abstains from alcohol and overcomes anxieties
Avoids social interaction	Actively works on social networks
Poor posture, body language	Good posture, confident body language
Gives to receive	Gives freely without expectation
Low confidence	Core character confidence
Seeks external validation	Internally secure, self-validating

AVERAGE MAN	ATTRACTIVE MAN
Avoids criticism	Actively seeks constructive feedback
Compares himself to others	Uses self-history to gauge progress
Permission-seeking	Self-starter
Approaches dating as a numbers game	Selective about women he genuinely likes
No dating strategy	Focuses on best mating market for himself
Passive	Active
Indecisive	Decisive
Purposeless	Purposeful
Scarcity	Abundance
Lives in their head	Lives in the real world
Stays in his comfort zone	Tests and increases the boundaries of his comfort zone
Quantity over quality	Quality over quantity
Blindly follows dating advice	Strategizes, picks best mating market for himself
Egotistical	Humble, self-aware
No goals	Purpose, lofty goals
Mumbling, monotonous	Dynamic, articulate

Printed in Great Britain
by Amazon